THE
WORLD *M*YTHOLOGY
SERIES

HEROES, GODS & EMPERORS
from
ROMAN MYTHOLOGY

HEROES, GODS & EMPERORS
from
ROMAN MYTHOLOGY

TEXT BY KERRY USHER
ILLUSTRATIONS BY JOHN SIBBICK

PETER BEDRICK BOOKS
NEW YORK

Peter Bedrick Books
2112 Broadway
New York, NY 10023

Published by agreement with Eurobook Ltd, England

Library of Congress Cataloging-in-Publication Data
Usher, Kerry.
   Heroes, gods & emperors from Roman mythology / text by
Kerry Usher; illustrations by John Sibbick
Originally published: New York : Schocken Books, 1984.
Includes index.
ISBN 0-87226-909-4
1. Mythology, Roman. 2. Gods, Roman. 3. Heroes—Rome.
4. Roman emperors. I. Sibbick, John. II. Title. III. Title:
Heroes, gods and emperors from Roman mythology.
[BL802.U83   1992]
398.2′0937—dc20   91-34713

Printed in Italy
5 4 3   96 97 98 99

THE AUTHOR
Kerry Usher has had a lifetime interest in Roman life and
customs, and studied Roman history as part of his Open
University BA degree course. He trained as a teacher at
Canterbury and was for three years headmaster of a rural
primary school. He has since worked as Administrator
of Chedworth Roman Villa in Gloucestershire, England.

THE ARTIST
John Sibbick studied art at Guildford School of Art and
worked as a general artist in a studio for some years.
He is now a full-time freelance artist and has specialized
in accurate reconstructions of life in the past.
Line drawings by Norman Bancroft-Hunt.

Contents

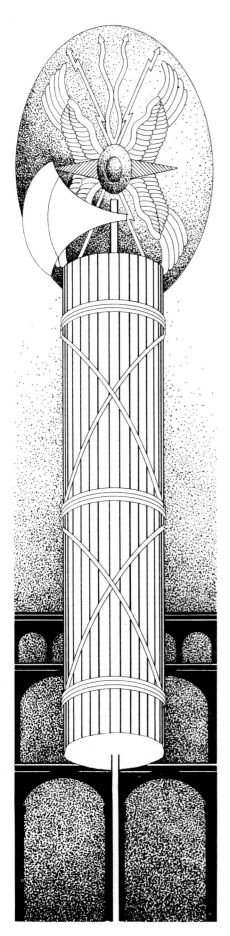

The city that conquered the world

The history of Rome is one of the most astonishing in the world. What began as a village of primitive huts beside the River Tiber some time in the eighth and seventh centuries BC grew to become a vast and splendid city with a mighty empire under its control. This empire, which encompassed several million square miles, was the greatest that the ancient world had ever seen.

According to modern historians the Rōman people had their origins somewhere in central Asia. In prehistoric times many ancient tribes moved gradually westwards into Europe. One group of tribes reached the north of the Italian peninsula some time before 1000 BC and moved south to their new homeland, fighting those already in occupation as they went. Among the newcomers was the tribe later called the Latins who settled in central Italy, on the plain of Latium.

The Italian peninsula must have been an inviting land to settle in, with its hospitable climate and many areas of rich farming land. Mild winters allowed cereal crops to be grown for an early summer harvest, while the gathering of olives and grapes was possible in the autumn. Plentiful pasture land encouraged the raising of animals.

Once the Latins had arrived in their new homeland it seems that one group settled the seven low hills beside the Tiber, the place which later became Rome. The people prospered and slowly grew in strength, gradually conquering neighbouring areas until the whole of Italy was under their control.

During this period of slow and painstaking expansion the Romans came into contact with a number of other peoples. Among them were the Etruscans, a powerful and civilized race who occupied a large part of northern Italy between the eighth and the fifth centuries BC. Another group which had moved in and occupied considerable areas of the peninsula, this time in the south, were the Greeks. The influence of both the Etruscans and the Greeks on the Latin tribes, and particularly on the early Romans, was enormous.

It seems that Rome was under direct Etruscan rule for much of the sixth century, the period when the Tarquins were kings. During that time Rome was transformed from a cluster of village settlements into a substantial city. The circular huts were replaced by Etruscan-style rectangular houses and temples built on strong stone foundations.

As Etruscan power waned the Romans decided to become independent. They expelled the king (Tarquinius Superbus) and established the Republic, the means by which Rome and her territories were governed for the next five hundred years.

Rome was fortunate because for a very long time it was never seriously threatened with domination by a foreign power. There were seldom times when it had to defend itself against a more powerful enemy, so usually victory was easy. This habit of being victorious made the Romans very self-assured. They went from strength to strength, moving from triumphs at home to a domination first of the Mediterranean world and then of the territories beyond.

However, all this was not achieved wholly without a struggle. When Rome challenged the power of the Greek settlements in southern Italy it became involved in a serious and costly war. The Romans were at last victorious but their control of the whole of Italy brought them into conflict with another major power—Carthage. More wars followed and Rome eventually managed to defeat the Carthaginians, this time to gain control of the western Mediterranean area.

Despite many social and political troubles at home, Roman territory continued to expand, right through Republican times and into the years of the early Empire. Gradually new areas were added by conquest and treaty until by the time of the Emperor Trajan, early in the second century AD, the Empire stretched from Britain and Germany in the north to Upper Egypt and the Atlas Mountains in the south, and from the Atlantic Ocean in the west to Armenia and the Caspian Sea in the east. Behind the conquering armies went governors, civil servants, engineers, architects and merchants. Every city became like Rome itself. Citizens in Spain and Gaul enjoyed the same privileges and bore the same responsibilities as those in the provinces of North Africa and Syria. All the widely scattered parts of the Empire were connected by a common system of government and by a vast road network. Slaves formed an efficient workforce and the leisured classes had time to cultivate the arts and to enjoy a life of luxury.

One remarkable achievement of the early Empire was the *Pax Romana* or Peace of Rome. From the time of the Emperor Augustus to that of the Emperor Marcus Aurelius, peace was the normal state of affairs throughout most of the provinces. Taxes were high but those taxes paid for an efficient army which kept the frontiers safe from invasion. Peace meant prosperity and citizens everywhere were grateful for its blessing.

As Roman power and influence spread to include so many of the great cultural centres of the past, so Rome itself could not fail to be influenced in a different way in return. The eastern provinces were steeped in the culture of Greece and this was inherited by Rome and made her own. The Romans developed a taste for much of the art, architecture and literature of ancient Greece. They also adopted many of its religious and philosophical beliefs, together with its elaborate mythology.

New trade links were set up and merchants in the ancient cities of the East were encouraged to send a great variety of luxury goods to Rome, among them silks, spices, bitumen and balsam. From these eastern provinces, too, came numerous teachers, doctors and artists.

The influence of Africa was also considerable. At that time North Africa and Egypt were remarkably productive and vast amounts of grain were sent to Rome each year. Of all the provinces it was Egypt which most stirred the Roman imagination. Apart from being a land rich in corn and gold it was also to many an eastern paradise of great antiquity, full of exotic animals and marvellous temples.

Obviously to conquer and maintain such a vast empire the Romans must have been an unusual people with unusual qualities. It is certain that their early history did much to shape their character. The earliest Romans were pioneer farmers who struggled hard to cultivate the land and to keep their enemies at a safe distance. They were hard-working, strong, disciplined and determined. They were also loyal, especially to their protective gods, to the community in which they lived and to the family. These qualities were inherited by later Romans and became part of their pattern of life.

One important part of the Roman character was a deep feeling for tradition and for the past.

Ancestors were always highly regarded and were believed to be constantly watching over the living. Reverence for ancestors was in fact at the very heart of Roman religious and social life. Stories about the brave deeds of past heroes of the race were always popular, mainly because they supported the belief that the Roman people were destined, from the beginning, to become great. Throughout the stories the Romans are shown to be unconquerable. It is they who win most of the battles, either because they have divine help or because they are braver or more steadfast than their opponents. The loss of a battle is seen as divine punishment for wrongdoing or as a reminder that they should be more watchful and disciplined. Repeatedly the same qualities are seen at work in making Rome great—courage, discipline and duty.

Although many of the stories the Romans told were carefully handed down by word of mouth from one generation to the next, others were specially written during the period when Augustus was Emperor (at the end of the first century BC). At that time writers such as Livy, Virgil and Horace drew on a wealth of legend, myth and folklore, as well as on historical fact, when they wrote about the great Roman past.

It is important to remember that the Romans were not makers of myth as the Greeks were. They did not think of their gods in human shape, neither did they worship them in the earliest times with the aid of temples and statues; rather they believed that objects and events had some kind of supernatural force. Their gods were only given human-like personalities after the Romans had made contact with the nearby Greek colonies and with their neighbours the Etruscans, who had also been influenced by Greek ideas. The old beliefs persisted for a long time, and with them a great deal of magic and superstition. Ritual and ceremony always played a very important part in Roman religion and also in everyday activities.

Roman religion remained firmly based on the family and the nation but as the city grew in power and influence, it required a more organized system of belief and the Romans adopted the Greek family of gods more or less unchanged, merging their personalities with characteristics of their own native powers and spirits. Stories of these superhuman beings were linked to legends of heroic ancestors and they came to be considered as truly Roman deities. The writers Virgil and Ovid knew and loved Italian folklore and legends. They realized that Rome had risen to greatness from humble beginnings and they believed that they could see a time of further greatness in the future. To celebrate the Roman achievement they produced a collection of stories written in the Greek manner but based on Italian themes. It is with the re-telling of many of these stories that this book is concerned.

The early chapters are about the gods and goddesses worshipped by the Romans. They explain many of the traditions and practices of Roman religion. Next there is a re-telling of the stories contained in Virgil's *Aeneid*, the account of how the gods planned the foundation of Rome.

The writings of the historian Livy provide the material for the next chapters, which tell of Romulus the legendary founder of Rome and of the kings who followed him. Then there are stories of famous heroes who each in turn contributed to Rome's greatness. Finally there are two collections of tales which, although written in the Greek manner, have very definite Italian settings.

The achievement of the Romans in the ancient world was truly remarkable, but their Empire could not last for ever. Eventually the pressure of attack from hordes of barbarian invaders from the east and the north, as well as weaknesses within the system of government, caused it to collapse. Although the Empire itself disappeared the Romans made such an impression on the areas that they conquered that clear traces of their ideas and methods, as well as their buildings and engineering projects, can still be found today. Rome also provided the setting for the early development of Christianity, the faith which survived the decline of the Roman state and which became the means by which much of that ancient culture was carried forward over the centuries. There are other survivals: the modern world owes a great deal to the world of Rome, for so much of its language, law, politics, architecture, art and literature is rooted there.

Gods of the countryside

From earliest times the Romans were farmers, living close to the land and dependent upon it for their survival and prosperity. These farming people were strongly aware of the supernatural in the world about them. The changes in the weather and in the seasons, the mysteries of pregnancy, birth and growth, all were beyond both understanding and control. They were both puzzling and awe-inspiring. It is easy, then, to understand how people came to believe that a magical power or force (something they called *numen*) was everywhere and in everything, showing itself in all the processes of life. Its influence was seen in all the activities of the farm, in the daily work within the family home and in the growth and development of children.

To understand this rather vague power better and also to ensure that its energy was directed in helpful ways, each of its actions was given a name. There was Vesta of the hearth-fire, Neptunus of the life-giving rain and spring-water, Terminus of the boundary-stone, Consus the Storer and many, many more.

For the most part these spirits or powers were kindly in their influence. They lived in the same house as the human family and on the same plot of land. If peace was made with them by means of prayer and sacrifice they would work for the benefit of all and would give protection against the unknown and dangerous powers that inhabited the wild places beyond the cultivated land. They would also ensure that the many and laborious tasks of the farmer would eventually be blessed with success.

To begin with all these powers which showed themselves in the activities of nature and of human life were rather vague beings without personalities. They simply made things happen or, more accurately, they were the happenings themselves. Gradually, however, ideas changed, especially under the influence of Greek culture with its rich mythology of colourful stories of gods and goddesses. In time the Romans, too, came to think of the powers in terms of deities with human-like forms. Two of these were Pomona and Vertumnus, whose story is told later in the book. Pomona was the goddess of fruit trees, especially of apple trees, while Vertumnus was the god of the changing seasons. There were others, like Flora

the goddess of flowers, who were given personalities, but few of them had stories told about them. In most cases the Greek gods, together with the stories the Greeks told about them, came to be identified with the native Italian or Roman ones. The Roman sky-god Jupiter was identified with Zeus, father of the Greek Olympian gods while the Roman corn-goddess Ceres became associated in most peoples' minds with the Greek goddess Demeter. Saturn, the Sower, who was probably a very ancient agricultural god, was identified with Cronos, leader of the Greeks' most ancient group of gods, the Titans. Mother Earth, too was a goddess common to both peoples. The Greeks called her Gaea while to the Romans she was known as Tellus Mater.

The Roman writer Varro began his book on agriculture by calling on the twelve deities who have a special interest in the process of farming. These Varro arranges in pairs. First he calls on Jupiter the Sky Father and Tellus the Earth Mother, who together rule over everything. Second he calls on Sol (the Sun) and Luna (the Moon), who regulate matters concerned with planting and harvesting. Third come Liber (Drink, especially wine) and Ceres (Food), the two things that sustain human life. Fourth there is Robigus, who keeps plants free from disease, and Flora, who ensures that plants flower. Then he calls on Minerva, the protectress of olive groves and Venus, the protectress of gardens. Lastly come Nympha, who produces water for the crops, and Bonus Eventus, the goddess who blesses the farmer's efforts with good fortune.

Varro also mentions two of the festivals held in honour of these country gods, the Robigalia for Robigus and the Floralia for Flora. There were many other festivals, held at different times of the year. Among them was the Ambarvalia. During this festival, a magic circle was drawn around the farm. On the appointed day, the farmer and all his people, wearing white clothes and wreaths of olive branches, led a male lamb three times around the boundary of the land. Then the lamb was sacrificed and the correct prayers recited. The deities Liber and Ceres were called upon to give plenty of food and drink in the coming year and to keep all evil away. After certain parts of the animal had been burned on the altar, everyone relaxed and enjoyed a feast. All this very serious activity was intended to encourage the good influences at work on the farm and shut out the bad ones.

The fields were not the only places to be under the protection of gods and goddesses. The wilder parts of the country, the hilly pastures and forests beyond the cultivated land, were also the haunt of deities. For example there was Faunus who, like the Greek Pan, was the god associated with shepherds, herdsmen and their animals. His fauns, spirits with the bodies of men and the legs of goats, lived with him in the woods. Another god of the wild places was Silvanus, 'He of the Forest', thought to be a particularly dangerous spirit. Another deity of the open countryside with its mountains and forests was Diana, an ancient Italian goddess who became identified with the Greek goddesses Artemis and Hecate. Her places of worship were usually in woods or groves of trees near springs or streams and her worshippers were usually women. Diana was also worshipped as the goddess of hunting and of the moonlit night.

Even after the growth of Rome as a city, the true Roman was always a farmer at heart, an idea which Varro is eager to support in his book. He discusses the long history of farming, saying that there were farmers on the earth long before there were city-dwellers. While it was the skill of men that made the building of cities possible, the countryside was the gift of the gods and was the true mother of all. The tillers of the land, he says, are the descendants of Saturn, the Sower, and their task is a good and useful one, for they work with the life-giving forces that once shaped the earth.

Many festivals like the Ambarvalia, which were originally connected with life in the countryside, found their way into the official worship of the great city of Rome. One annual festival with ancient beginnings was that celebrated in Rome during February and called the *Lupercalia*. Originally it seems to have been concerned with the driving away of wolves which attacked flocks and herds, but in later times its purpose was to increase fertility and drive out evil spirits from the city.

Gods of the family

Always at the heart of Roman religion was the family, the smallest group within the community. Like any other section of society, it needed divine help for the success of its life and work. The person responsible for ensuring that help was forthcoming was the head of the family and it was he who had to carry out the necessary rituals. These took place in the family home, or close to it, usually at the household shrine or *Lararium*. This shrine was like a cupboard which stood in a corner of the main room and contained small statues representing the household gods, the Lares. The Lares were the spirits of the family's dead ancestors and they took a continuing interest in its living members. The family would pray each day to their Lares, offering a small gift of incense, food or wine at the same time.

Other Lares were believed to live outside the house in the surrounding fields. Land was traditionally divided up into regular plots, and the place where four such plots or small-holdings met was called a *compitum*. At that point a small shrine was usually erected, open on all four sides so that the Lar of each farm or plot could enter and leave it freely. Four altars were set up around it. At the end of each farming year the festival of Compitalia was celebrated and a plough would be hung on the shrine, together with a woollen doll for every free person in the household and a woollen ball for every slave. A sacrifice on the next day was followed by a holiday. The ceremony was intended to bring life and health to both the land and to the people who lived and worked upon it.

In towns and cities, blocks of houses replaced the plots of land and shrines dedicated to the local Lares were set up at crossroads. Each year the families living nearby gathered for a three-day festival which began with the sacrifice of a hen. By all accounts it was a really riotous occasion.

Since Lares were regarded as protectors of crossroads it is hardly surprising that they were also believed to protect roads, as well as those who travelled in any way, including sailors and soldiers. Just as the family Lares guarded the home and the farm so these other Lares were thought to protect Roman territory and its citizens everywhere.

The other deities of the household which were worshipped by the family were the Penates—the powers that protected the *penus* or store-cupboard—and Vesta the hearth-goddess. These were honoured each day with prayers and offerings while at festivals, garlands of flowers adorned the altar of the Penates and the hearth.

The first houses consisted of just a single room in which the whole family lived. It contained the hearth and the lararium and also the marriage-bed. Even when houses became more complex, with several rooms, the tradition of having a bed in the main living-room continued so that in later times you would still expect to see it there, just opposite the door. No human ever used this bed, however, for it belonged to the Genius (literally 'the begetter'), the family spirit or numen which enabled one generation to follow the next. The Genius can be thought of as the spirit head of the family, continuing its name and protecting it from danger. The father of each family was believed to have his own Genius, his link with his ancestors and with those who would follow him.

Perhaps the Genius shared the sacred bed with another occupant for although a Genius was something that always belonged to a man, a woman had a female counterpart, her Juno.

The idea of Genius was eventually taken beyond the family, for it could be said of a legion, a town or a community of traders that each had its own Genius. Rome certainly had its own guiding and protecting Genius. Each of the Emperors, from Augustus onwards, had his Genius and it was this, rather than the Emperor himself, that was the object of worship.

Another part of the family home which was believed to be protected by a god was its outer door. This doorway and all its parts (posts, lintel, threshold and the door itself with its hinges) were charged with numen or super-natural power, and going through it had great magical significance. Opening and closing the door and walking through the doorway could have good or evil consequences, depending on the will of the god Janus, or Doorway, who lived at everyone's doorway and indeed at the gates of towns and cities. In Rome, Janus gained great importance and had a temple in the Forum fitted with huge gates which always stood open in times of war and closed when peace returned. Janus was symbolized by a head with two faces, looking in opposite directions. His month was January, the time of beginnings.

Life's beginnings, too, had a very special significance. It seems that many deities were believed to be present at every birth, all helping Juno, the great goddess of women, as she attended the mother. The newly-born child was placed on the ground and then lifted up by its father. Evil spirits were driven from the house and thank-offerings made to the gods to ensure their protective influences.

Children, once past the baby stage, were expected to help their parents in the performance of the family rituals. A boy would help his father, learning the prayers and ceremonies concerned with the worship of the household gods, while a girl would help her mother to look after the hearth and honour Vesta its goddess. At about the age of fourteen children came of age and special family ceremonies marked the event. A boy wore a special charm during childhood and at his coming-of-age ceremony this was dedicated to the household gods while the purple-edged toga he had worn as a child was replaced by a plain white one. Marriage was the ceremony which marked a girl's entry into adulthood. Inevitably there were many rituals that had to be performed at a marriage to ward off evil spirits, especially during the bride's journey from the house of her father to that of her husband. Other rituals ensured good luck and happiness in the future.

An ancient festival celebrated each year by every family was the Saturnalia. This was held in honour of Saturn, the Sower, a god of seedtime and harvest, and took place during the last half of December. After a visit to the temple of Saturn, everyone enjoyed a feast of food and wine. Slaves were given their freedom during the festival and their masters served them at table. People exchanged simple gifts and amused themselves with party games. In later times this festival was replaced by the Christian feast of Christmas, but many of the old customs remained. In Roman days, the Saturnalia was a time when everyone remembered the far-off Golden Age when Saturn ruled the land and all men lived together in peace.

Gods of city and state

Although Rome began as a small tribal community, it grew in time to be a teeming city with a vast area under its control. By the time Augustus became Emperor (towards the end of the first century BC) about a million people lived there, mostly crowded into thousands of smelly, badly-built blocks of flats. For the majority of people conditions were difficult. Apart from overcrowding there was a shortage of houses and jobs, rents were high, the streets were constantly congested with horses, chariots and pedestrians, the air was polluted with smoke and sanitation was poor. In fact, Rome suffered from many of the problems which beset cities in our own time. Since Rome was the centre of government and trade, it was also the home of many rich and influential people. In addition to the squalid tenement blocks occupied by the poor, the city contained splendid public buildings including temples, baths, theatres and palaces. In the countryside around were magnificent villas, the country estates of the rich.

As Rome grew in importance and power, so did its gods. Many of the deities who had been revered by the family and by the early farming communities became gods and goddesses of the city and then of the whole Roman state. Vesta was one of these, for this goddess of the family hearth-fire was adopted as guardian of the holy fire in the city of Rome. Unlike most of the other gods and goddesses, Vesta was never represented by a statue of any sort, for she was always thought of as being the hearth-fire itself. Her fire was relit every March and then tended for the rest of the year by her priestesses, the Vestal Virgins. Within the circular shrine where the fire burned was the city's store cupboard in which a number of sacred and precious objects were kept, guarded by the Penates of the Roman people. Both Vesta and the Penates were thought of as guardian deities of the Roman state: the holy fire of Vesta was the hearth-fire of the city and, indeed of the Empire. Eventually temples in her honour, containing her undying fire, were set up in cities throughout the Roman world. If the fire ever went out the Romans recognized it as a very serious portent and expected disaster to follow, for her cult came to symbolize the undying power of Rome.

Apart from Vesta the principal goddesses of the Roman state were

19

Juno, Minerva, Ceres, Diana and Venus, while the chief gods were Jupiter, Mars, Apollo, Mercury and Neptune. Temples, priests and special rituals were provided by the state to honour these deities, leaving the ordinary citizen with little part to play in official worship.

The temples, where worship usually took place, were impressive, elegant buildings, each containing a large statue of its particular god or goddess. Many of the ceremonies, performed by the cult priests, took place outside the temples at special altars.

Although the public took little part in the rituals of worship, they were very much involved in the frequent festivals that were held in honour of the various gods. These festivals were also holidays and were usually the occasion for spectacular games, held in special arenas and circuses. In early times athletic displays and chariot races were the main events but later these were replaced by gladiatorial combats, where professionals fought each other to the death or struggled with captives and even wild animals.

As important as the official priests were two groups of men, the augurs and the haruspices, who were responsible for interpreting signs believed to be sent by the gods. The augurs were concerned with examining the behaviour of birds and of thunder and lightning in order to discover the gods' will in matters of importance, while the haruspices inspected the livers of sacrificed animals for the same purpose. Both were consulted before any important state decision was made or if some unexpected natural phenomenon occurred.

Of all the gods and goddesses so far mentioned the most important and powerful was Jupiter, lord of the Sky. He was very much like the Greek god Zeus and so became completely identified with him. As the sky-god he was the bringer of light, the cause of dawn and of the moon's shining. He also controlled the weather, sending thunder and lightning, as well as life-giving rain. Lightning was seen as a particularly powerful sign of Jupiter's presence and things struck by lightning, especially certain trees, were considered to be sacred to him and in his possession. Jupiter's symbols were the thunder-bolt and the eagle, both of which were

carried on the standards of the Roman legions.

In earliest times certain stones were thought to be thunderbolts and these became associated with Jupiter as the god of thunder. In Rome a stone called the rain stone was used at a special festival in honour of Jupiter as rain god, to summon rain. Stones were also used when solemn promises and treaties were made, for Jupiter was the god of oaths, who watched over truth and justice. In this capacity he was seen to have the laws of nations, especially those of Rome, under his special protection. He was regarded as patron and lord of all that was Roman and as the defender of the people.

Like Rome's other principal deities, Jupiter had his own priest and priestess who were responsible for the special ceremonies held in honour of the god. His main shrine in the city of Rome was on the Capitol and was dedicated to him as Jupiter Optimus Maximus ('Best and Greatest'), just one of his many titles. In the central room of the temple stood the god's statue, showing him as a triumphant general, while two other rooms were dedicated to Rome's chief goddesses, Juno and Minerva.

Juno, as wife of Jupiter, was the Queen of Heaven and of heavenly light, especially of moonlight. She was identified with the Greek goddess Hera. As Juno the Bringer of Light she was worshipped from earliest times. She was the goddess of the beginnings of all the months and also of birth. Indeed, she was particularly worshipped by women, who looked to her as their special guardian. Her most important festival was the Matronalia, celebrated on the first day of March each year by the women of the city. At this time the goddess was represented as a mother with a flower in one hand and a baby in the other. The women prayed at Juno's temple and left offerings, then returned home to receive gifts from the men and to wait on the slaves, just as the men did at the Saturnalia (the yearly feast of the god Saturn).

Juno was also the goddess of marriage and was seen to bless its many aspects. Her month of June was always a favourite time to get married.

Another important goddess of the Roman state and a consort of Jupiter was Minerva. Like her Greek counterpart, Pallas Athena, she was

queen of wisdom and the arts and so was worshipped by craftsmen, artists of every kind, doctors, teachers and schoolchildren. Her festival, in March, was the Quinquatrus and was celebrated by all who regarded her as their protector. Schoolchildren were given a holiday for the festival and teachers received their yearly pay at the same time, for the celebrations marked the end of one school year and the beginning of the next.

Apart from the temple on the Capitol which she shared with Jupiter and Juno, Minerva had a temple on the Caelian Hill, as well as one on the Aventine which was the official meeting place of actors and poets.

After Jupiter, the greatest god among the ancient Italians was Mars, in whose honour the Roman month Martius was named. Mars had very ancient connections with both agriculture and war. In the beginning he was called upon as a fertilizing god to bless the fields and animals and to keep away anything that did harm. A horse was usually sacrificed to him to ensure the growth of the seed after the autumn sowing.

Perhaps Mars became associated with war because both the farming year and the fighting year began in the spring, during March in fact. As the god of war his symbols were the wolf, the woodpecker and the lance. When war broke out, which it often did as the Romans expanded their empire, the god was called with the words 'Mars, awake!' and the holy shields were struck with the holy lance. During the fighting which followed, many sacrifices were offered to ensure his blessing and support.

According to the ancient legend of the founding of Rome, Mars was the father of the twins Romulus and Remus and it was he who protected them in their infancy by causing one of his sacred animals, a she-wolf, to look after them. The Romans believed that this divine interest in their beginnings gave them their great success in war and conquest and Mars was seen as the god responsible for the Roman army's many victories. The Emperor Augustus even gave him a new title as 'Mars the Avenger'.

Very closely connected with Mars was Quirinus, originally the war god of a tribe called the Sabines, who were neighbours of the

It is not possible to finish an account of the gods of the Roman state without mentioning Venus, especially as she appears frequently in some of the stories which follow. Her origins are very obscure and it is not clear how or when she became associated with the Greek love goddess Aphrodite. Whatever her original nature, she gained a place of importance in Roman mythology and the early Roman Emperors, the Julii, and Julius Caesar himself, claimed to be descended from her through her mortal son Aeneas. She was given the title Venus Genetrix, or Mother of the Roman people. As Venus Genetrix she had a temple in the Forum (built in 46 BC) and games were held each year in her honour. As goddess of love she was called upon to smooth the path of love and to bring happiness to those whom she favoured.

One deity to gain great popularity both in Rome and far beyond the city limits was the goddess of luck or chance, Fortuna. Her shrine was on the banks of the river Tiber, a few miles from the city, and every year on 24 June, crowds of people went there to celebrate her festival. Unlike most cults this one was open to all, both slave and free, and the festival provided a great opportunity for a day of entertainment either on the river or at its edge. Fortuna was worshipped under many titles, such as Fortune of the Men, of the Women, of Maidens, of the Emperor, of Rome, of the Family—of every type of person who might benefit from her powers.

Rome, as the city that ruled so much of the known world, had its own special goddess called Dea Roma. Her worship was usually connected with that of the Emperors. Rome's river, the Tiber, also had its own highly honoured god, Tiberinus. There are two stories connected with this god. One tells how an old king called Tiber was drowned while swimming across the river, which was in those days known as the Albula. When he died he became the river's god, giving his name to it at the same time. The other story links the river with Rome's founder Romulus and his brother Remus. It is said that their mother was thrown into the waters as a punishment but was saved from death by the god Tiberinus, who claimed her as his queen and made her goddess of the river.

Romans. In later times Quirinus became identified with Romulus, the founder of Rome, who was himself believed to have become a god after his death. Quirinus had his own temple on the Quirinal Hill as well as his own priests and festival. Interestingly, Quirinus shows a different side of a war god's character—his willingness to stop fighting and agree on terms of peace.

Another important god in the Roman world was Mercury, the patron of businessmen and traders. He was likened to the Greek Hermes, the messenger of the gods, while another god, Apollo, was adopted straight from the Greeks without even changing his name. He was not, however, considered to be very important in Rome until the time of the Emperor Augustus. Apparently Apollo appeared to Augustus during a battle and assured him that he would be victorious. The Emperor immediately set up temples to Apollo as the god of peace and civilization and also of success in the new social order that Augustus was working hard to create.

Spirits of the Underworld

In common with many other peoples the Romans were very concerned about death and with the welfare of those who had died. The dead were thought to bring some of the wrong kind of numen to the living. This was a sort of ill-luck and could only be dispelled if the correct rituals were observed. These rituals also ensured that the soul of the dead person made a safe journey from the world of the living to that of the 'good people' or Manes.

The body of the dead person was carefully prepared, then carried on a bier to the place of burial, followed by the family in procession. The roadsides were commonly used as burial grounds, especially those just outside towns and cities. Sometimes people were buried on their own land, perhaps at the edge of a field. Often the body was simply buried in the ground but usually it was burned on a pyre first and the ashes buried. It was the act of burying, or putting underground, that was important, for unless this was done the spirit of the dead person might haunt his home and family and continue to bring them ill-luck.

Fire was believed to be powerful against the bad influences brought by death. That is probably why bodies were burned and why torches were carried at funerals. Once the burial had taken place the house of the dead person was ritually purified, the family mourned for nine days and a sacrifice was offered to the family Lares.

The funerals of important people were the most elaborate. Usually the houses of such people contained, on permanent display, wax masks of the family ancestors. At funerals these would be worn or carried by actors dressed to represent those ancestors. This impressed the onlookers, but also had a serious ritual function. It meant that the former members of the family were seen to be present to escort the dead person to his place of burial, which would probably be an elaborate family tomb just outside the city. With very few exceptions burials did not take place within built-up areas.

The dead, once buried, were by no means neglected, for every year during February (the month of purification) they were remembered at the Parentalia or festival of parents. This was traditionally a time when graves and tombs were visited and decorated with flowers. It was usual during a burial to leave food and drink within the tomb, and at each Parentalia this was renewed. Without it the Manes were liable to become very hungry and might emerge from their graves.

During May there was another festival concerned with the spirits of the dead. This was the Lemuria, the time when all the evil spirits (*lemures*) were believed to haunt their old homes, usually with disastrous results. The poet Ovid wrote an account of the ritual which every householder performed to send the ghosts back to the Underworld. He rose at midnight, washed his hands, then placed nine black beans in his mouth. As he walked barefoot about the house he spat the beans out one at a time with the magic words: 'With these I ransom me and mine'. The ghosts were thought to follow him and eat the beans. Still without looking behind him, the man washed his hands again, beat a gong and spoke another spell nine times. When he finally looked round the ghosts had gone!

There is very little in old Italian tradition that explains the exact nature of the place where the spirits of the dead were thought to go and very little concerning the gods and goddesses who ruled over them. The Greeks, on the other hand, were far more definite and it was from them that the Romans borrowed many ideas about the Underworld and its gods. Several names were given to the god who ruled the lower world. One was Orcus, derived from the Greek word *horkos* meaning 'oath'; he was thought to carry the dead off to his dark, mysterious realm where he kept them imprisoned. Dis Pater was another name for the same character, and he was also called Hades and Pluto, all names of Greek origin. But Pluto was not just the gloomy lord of the Underworld. *Ploutos* in Greek means 'wealth', so Pluto, 'the Wealthy One', was also lord of the earth's treasures.

It is not surprising, therefore, that Pluto's name should be linked with two important goddesses of fertility, Ceres, the corn-goddess (called Demeter by the Greeks) and her daughter Proserpine (Persephone). In the Greek story, which the Romans adopted, Proserpine was gathering flowers in the fields one day when Pluto passed by in his chariot. Seeing her beauty, he was determined to take her as his wife and, snatching her up, he carried her off to the Underworld in his chariot. Ceres searched everywhere for her daughter, mad with grief at her disappearance. She was so distracted that she forgot her duties as a goddess: the crops failed to grow without her guidance, trees and flowers shed their leaves, the land became empty and barren as she mourned.

At last Ceres discovered where her daughter was being held prisoner and sent the messenger of the gods to plead with Pluto for her safe return. Reluctantly Pluto agreed, but only, he said, if Proserpine had not eaten anything during her captivity. By mistake, she had swallowed seven tiny pomegranate pips and because of this it was agreed that she must spend three months of every year in the kingdom of the dead, returning to the upper world each spring. From that time on the earth knew winter, for while her daughter was away, Ceres turned her face from the land. Only when Proserpine returned did the flowers bloom again and the crops begin to push their way through the cold earth.

There were many places in the ancient world which were believed to be the entrance to the realm of Pluto. According to Roman tradition it could be entered near a volcanic lake in southern Italy called Avernus, not far from Cumae.

Roman descriptions of what it was like in the Underworld rely very much on details from Greek myths. Apart from being the place where Pluto and Proserpine ruled supreme, it was also believed to be the haunt of monsters, ghosts and all the evils of the world, as well as being the spirit home of all who have ever lived.

After death every soul entered this vast and eerie realm beneath the earth and then had to be ferried across a wide river. The ferryman, called Charon, demanded a small coin from each soul in exchange for the ride. For this reason a coin was usually placed on the tongue of every dead person before their funeral.

On the far side of the river the entrance to the realms beyond was guarded by Cerberus, a fierce watch-dog with three heads. Further on, the road divided, one way leading to Tartarus, a terrible place of punishment, the other going on by way of Pluto's palace to Elysium, the land of eternal light where all those who had lived good lives enjoyed happiness for evermore.

Gods from the East

The established religion of Rome was a rather unexciting affair. It was solemn and respectable but demanded little of the ordinary worshipper. Above all it lacked a real sense of mystery. The gods were thought of as being concerned only with fertility, the weather, war and, more particularly, with the family and with the Roman state. The rewards for belief and for observing the rituals were restricted very much to this life, for death was seen as the end of a person's useful existence. After death the shades merely hovered around in the shadowy realm of Dis, perhaps occasionally returning to trouble the living.

As the Empire expanded, the Romans came into contact with faiths different from their own and usually they tolerated them. Even before Rome became conqueror of the world, however, the influence of other religions and ideas had been felt. The greatest influence was from Greece but there were others, mainly from the area which we today call the Near East. Several eastern cults arrived in Rome, some as early as the second century BC, bringing with them faiths that became popular immediately. Among the most important was the worship of the 'Great Mother'.

The year 205 BC marked a turning point in the war against the Carthaginians, a people based on the city of Carthage, near present-day Tunis. The Carthaginians were powerful in the western Mediterranean and fiercely resisted Roman attempts to take control. Battles were fought both on land and at sea and Rome had already won many victories. However, the Carthaginian commander Hannibal still controlled part of Italy and the people of Rome felt threatened. They were so afraid that it was decided to consult the Sibylline books. These ancient books contained prophecies but were only read when there was a real emergency. Now they revealed that the enemy could only be defeated if the Great Mother, the goddess Cybele, was brought from Pessinus in Asia Minor.

Cybele's image at Pessinus was in the form of a shapeless black stone representing the face of a silver statue of the goddess. We do not know how the Pessinians reacted when they had to give it up but it was duly taken to Rome and housed in a temple on the Palatine where it remained for over five hundred years. Not long after its arrival, Hannibal and his army left Italian soil.

Cybele was just one name by which the Great Mother Goddess was known in ancient times. Many peoples have had many names for this mother of the gods and of all creation; the loving and protective force at work in nature and in human life. However, the Goddess Cybele had another aspect, for she was also concerned with all that was magical and mysterious, with forces that were beyond understanding. It was this aspect that was missing in the Roman religion of the family and the state. Juno was certainly something of a mother goddess, but she had little power beside the warrior gods and she was concerned more with the practical aspects of human life than with the forces of the unknown. Even the numen which was thought to be present in the activities of life was a very impersonal force and made no demands on the believer.

While the cult of Cybele was not exactly welcomed enthusiastically in Rome, the people felt that the right action had been taken. Not everyone approved of the rites and ceremonies which were part of the worship of the goddess, and steps were taken to make the cult respectable and Roman.

Cybele was not usually worshipped on her own. She had a companion deity called Attis who, according to legend, was her favourite. In a fit of madness, caused by Cybele's jealousy, he wounded himself with a knife and died as a result. After death Attis was reborn, to be reunited with Cybele. It was these legendary events which were copied in the worship of the goddess. At her spring festival a freshly-cut pine tree was carried in procession to represent the dead Attis. A period of mourning followed. Then came the Day of Blood when the cult followers danced madly, then whipped themselves and even slashed themselves with knives, just as Attis had done. After a further night of mourning came the Hilaria when the worshippers went wild with joy in celebration of the god's return to life. Later the image of the goddess was washed with great ceremony in the river.

Another ritual was called the *taurobolium* or bull-sacrifice. Through this a believer could become 'born again' by means of a blood sacrifice. The worshipper stood in a pit while a bull was slaughtered on a platform above. The blood ran down to cover his body and he emerged as a 'new person', 'reborn' as Attis himself.

Obviously there were other rituals and ceremonies for those who became believers, but because this was essentially a mystery religion their details were kept secret. However, it seems certain that the worshippers of Cybele and Attis believed themselves to be taking part in the great drama of death and rebirth, and of the return of the human soul to the company of the gods. In contrast with the traditional Roman religion the worship of the Great Mother provided something very personal.

For those who wanted a personal faith of this sort there were other possibilities, among them the Egyptian cult of Isis. In the early days of the Empire the Romans became fascinated by the great antiquity and strangeness of Egypt and there was a fashion for all things Egyptian, including religion. The worship of Isis had already spread very widely through the Mediterranean countries, reaching Italy around the fourth century BC. It remained popular in Rome for centuries, despite several attempts by the government to have it banned. The cult appealed to the poorer classes of Roman society as well as to the many foreign residents in Italy. Eventually the ruling class and even the emperors adopted the worship of Isis, and that was enough to ensure its lasting popularity.

Isis was really the Egyptian version of the Great Mother goddess; another Cybele in fact. Like Cybele, she was often worshipped with a companion god. In her case it was Osiris, a god who died and rose again, just like Attis. According to the ancient legend Osiris and Isis were brother and sister as well as husband and wife and left their heavenly realm to live on earth. Osiris became a great king but his brother, Seth, grew jealous of him and murdered him. Seth shut Osiris inside a coffin and threw it into the River Nile. Isis, wild with grief, searched furiously until she found her husband's body but Seth discovered what had happened, cut the body into fourteen pieces and scattered them

of Isis are contained in a book called *The Golden Ass* written in the second century AD by Apuleius. The book tells the story of a young man who is turned into an ass by the use of a charm. He can only return to his human shape by eating fresh roses, and while searching for this remedy has many entertaining adventures. Eventually Isis appears to him, directing him to eat the roses carried by the priest in her spring festival on the following day. His transformation takes place as promised and the young man becomes a devoted worshipper. Later he is initiated into the mysteries of the Isis cult. Without telling any of the secrets, Apuleius describes some of his experiences; how he went to the very edge of death, saw the sun at midnight and worshipped the gods at close quarters. After the ceremony he appeared to the congregation dressed like the sun-god. As a priest of Isis he spent the rest of his life serving the goddess and protected by her. It is not difficult to understand why so many people found the cult of the Egyptian deities so attractive.

Another of the mystery religions widely accepted in Roman times was Mithraism, a belief which had its origins in ancient Persia. It was based on the idea that the forces of good and evil are constantly at war. Although good will eventually win, the two forces are so equally matched that the struggle is a fierce one in which humans play their part, especially on the side of good.

The god Mithras, from whom the faith obtained its name, was a deity of light and truth. There are many myths connected with him but the most important is the one which tells of the sacrifice of a bull. On the orders of the sun-god, Mithras reluctantly slaughtered a sacred bull and as the bull died the world came into being and time was born. The cloak of Mithras became the heavens, studded with stars and planets, while from the bull came all the plants and living creatures, the four elements and the seasons. The shedding of blood brought great blessings which the power of evil tried to prevent. The struggle between good and evil which began then will continue until the end of time.

Our knowledge of the practices and beliefs of

throughout the land. Isis again searched and recovered all but one of the pieces. Osiris then returned from death and fathered his son, Horus, to be his avenger.

As a god, Osiris became ruler of the dead, but he was not just that; he was also believed to be concerned with the living and with the processes that supported life both on earth and in the realm beyond. The Egyptians had a fervent belief in human survival after death. In the rituals practised by his worshippers, the death and resurrection of Osiris played a very important part.

In the Roman world it was Isis, the eternal wife and mother, who was the more popular of the two Egyptian gods. She was easily identified with any number of other mother-goddesses such as Cybele, Hera, Juno, Aphrodite and Athena, all familiar in the ancient world. Her worship, with its secrecy and its mysteries, appealed to a deep, personal need felt by many, while it lacked the savagery of the rites of Cybele.

Some details of what it meant to be a follower

Mithraism is not very detailed. Like other mystery religions it had many secrets and we can only guess at what these were. However, it does seem to have attracted a large number of believers, all of them men and most of them soldiers. It was a faith which demanded a great deal and it stressed the need to fight against evil. There were definite rules of conduct laid down and also a series of tests of determination and courage.

Because Mithraism was particularly popular with soldiers it found its way to the furthest outposts of the empire. In Britain, for example, the remains of a number of Mithraic temples have been discovered. Apart from one found in London the temples are all on military sites— one near the fort at Segontium (Caernarvon) in Wales and three on Hadrian's Wall in northern England.

It is clear that all these mystery cults have certain things in common. The god or goddess is friendly to the human race and also suffers, in many cases dying and rising to a new life; the believer has to go through special ceremonies of initiation; a strict code of behaviour has to be observed; believers are promised a happy life after death; and all the deities worshipped have strong connections with heavenly bodies, especially the sun.

It was in this world, where mystery cults were such a common feature, that Christianity had its beginnings.

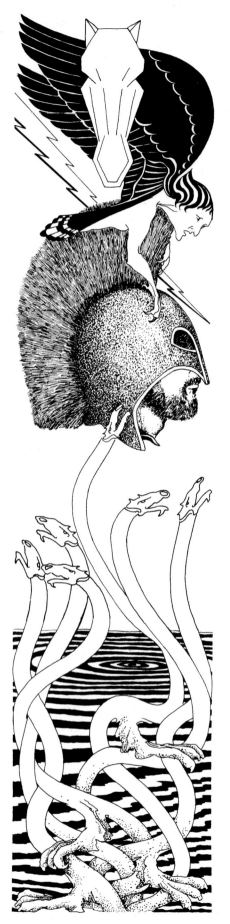

The story of Aeneas

'I tell a tale of war and of a hero. This hero was chosen by Fate to be an exile and it was he who first set out from Troy and reached the Lavinian shore of Italy. Throughout his journey, by land and by sea, he was beset by troubles, tormented by the heavenly powers because of the anger of Juno. In war he suffered greatly, too, until at last he managed to found the city of Lavinium, a home for the ancient gods of his race. It was from this city that the whole Latin nation sprang, the kings of Alba and of Rome itself.'

It was with these words that Virgil began his epic poem *The Aeneid*, the story of Aeneas, Prince of Troy. Troy itself was a city in a country called Phrygia, which is now part of modern Turkey. The history of its long war against the Greeks was well known to the Romans and they were proud to trace their ancestry back to Aeneas, a Trojan who escaped when his city was destroyed and made his way to Italy to become the father-founder of the Roman people.

The Roman poet Publius Vergilius Maro, known to us simply as Virgil, began the task of writing his *Aeneid* in about 30 BC. It was his last work and when he died eleven years later it was still not completed. Just before he died, he asked his friends to burn the unfinished poem but they knew how good it was and, fortunately, persuaded him to change his mind.

The Aeneid is usually described as an epic because it is a long poem telling a story of superhuman beings, or 'heroes', who are in direct contact with the gods. In writing it, Virgil was following an ancient tradition. The oldest known story of this kind is the Babylonian *Epic of Gilgamesh*, written down over 4,000 years ago. Two other very old and very important epics are *The Iliad* and *The Odyssey*, both by the Greek poet Homer. Like *The Aeneid* these both deal with the Trojan war and the events that followed it—but very much from the Greek point of view.

The Aeneid is a fast-moving story full of adventure, romance and tragedy. It is also an account of a voyage and includes many authentic details of navigation and geography, while its second half is full of vivid descriptions of armies at war. Included, too, is the strange story of Aeneas' journey to the Underworld, the realm of the dead, where he learns about the future greatness of his people. It can be read just as a good and exciting story, but it is also much more than that, for it has many hidden meanings.

Virgil's aim was to write the story of Rome's greatest ancestor, a man who was not only the son of a goddess but who had also lived through the events of the great war of Troy. There were in existence several ancient legends about this character, and these Virgil used with great skill and imagination. It seems very likely that the legends were based on events which actually took place in the distant past. Perhaps a group of people did migrate from the area near Troy in Asia Minor to the western Mediterranean, and perhaps they did settle in Italy, leaving some of their number in the various places that they visited on the way. Sadly, we can never know for certain.

Not all the characters in the story of Aeneas are human or even superhuman. The gods and goddesses play important parts as the drama unfolds. Venus, the goddess of love, is always anxious to protect her son Aeneas while Juno, the Queen of the gods, constantly opposes him. Jupiter tries to keep the peace and even Neptune makes occasional appearances. It seems that Virgil had a very strong belief that the affairs of men were influenced by the heavenly powers. For him this was as true in his own time as it was in the far distant days of Aeneas.

Aeneas first appears in Virgil's story on the night when Troy is finally destroyed by the Greeks, but to learn more about him and about his father Anchises it is necessary to delve back into Greek mythology. Anchises was king of the Dardanians (a people who were neighbours of the Trojans) and when young he loved to wander among the mountains, far from the city. One night he took shelter in a deserted herdsman's hut high on Mount Ida. Apparently Jupiter wanted to humiliate his daughter Venus by making her fall in love with a mortal, and the handsome Anchises seemed the perfect choice. Venus had watched the young king all that day and had, as Jupiter decreed, fallen madly in love with him. During the night, disguised as a human princess, she crept into the hut and shared Anchises' bed. Before they parted next day Venus told him who she was and promised

to protect him and the son she would bear him, on condition that he kept their meeting a secret. Eventually the goddess gave birth to Aeneas but Anchises could not resist boasting about what had happened. Jupiter was so angry that he threw a deadly thunderbolt at the King, but Venus, who still loved him, deflected the missile so that it struck the ground beside him. The shock was sufficient to cripple Anchises, and from that day he walked with a limp.

Later Aeneas and his fellow Dardanians became involved in the Trojan war and it is with that great event that the real story begins.

For ten long years the Greeks and Trojans had been at war. They fought for the possession of a beautiful woman, some thought the most beautiful woman on earth. Her name was Helen. Paris, the son of King Priam of Troy, had fallen in love with Helen while on a visit to her husband Menelaus and had persuaded her to leave home and sail away with him.

Menelaus was furious. He was king of Sparta, a powerful man with the means to take a terrible revenge. He called together his friends and allies, with their fleets and war hosts, and sailed in pursuit.

The city of Troy was rich and influential, with large territories under its command. It stood on a hill near the shore of the Hellespont, the narrow stretch of water between Europe and Asia. It was on this shore, below the walls of Troy, that the Greeks beached their huge fleet and swiftly built a camp for the besieging army.

The two forces were equally matched and the war dragged on with no end in sight and little chance of victory for either side. Paris refused to return Helen to Menelaus and many quarrels broke out among the Trojan leaders because of her. People on both sides grew sick of the war and desperately wanted it to end.

Yet the fighting went on, until one fateful day. It dawned brightly enough, like all the rest, and as usual the Trojans looked out towards the shore where the Greeks had made their camp. What they saw amazed them, for the shoreline settlement, usually alive with activity, was a smouldering and deserted ruin. The ships that were usually drawn up on the beach had vanished. The sea, too, was empty. But the

Greeks had not taken everything with them. Standing on the plain below the city stood a huge horse made of wood.

Thinking that the war was over, the Trojans were overjoyed. The city gates were opened and everyone swarmed out across the shore to where the massive horse stood, silent and alone. What the Trojans did not realize, although some of them suspected it, was that hidden in the cavernous belly of the horse were the Greeks' bravest and strongest warriors, waiting in silent ambush. A great debate began among the people. 'It is an offering to Athena,' said some, 'so it should be taken into the city and placed in her temple.'
'The Greeks are not to be trusted,' argued others. 'This horse is just another of their tricks! Let us burn it here on the shore.'

The argument raged back and forth until at last the crowd was swayed in favour of preserving the horse. Ropes and wheels were brought so that the wooden beast could be dragged into the city. The gateway nearest the sea was partly dismantled to make room as it was towed through, and it was pulled on right to the inmost citadel of Troy. There it stood at last, before the temple of Pallas Athena. Everywhere was decked with bright garlands and great festivities began to celebrate the longed-for peace. No-one seemed aware of the danger that lurked within the horse. Already their doom was sealed.

Sleep came quickly to the people of Troy after the great excitement of the day. The night was still and intensely dark. Nothing stirred within the city, but out to sea, just out of sight of land, the Greek fleet waited, and on a given signal stole back to the shore. The men inside the horse left their hiding place and opened the gates ready for the attack. Troy stood at the mercy of the Greeks.

Among those sleeping within the city were Aeneas and his family. Like everyone else they were woken by sounds unfamiliar within the city walls—the angry crackle of flames, the noise of battle and the cries of people in anguish. The Greeks had entered the city unchallenged and now they were ruthlessly ransacking and killing everywhere. The destruction was terrible. The Trojan men, still drowsy and unprepared, desperately strapped on their armour and snatched up their weapons, hoping to rout the invaders. But there was little that they could do. Fire had taken a firm hold everywhere. People ran screaming from their burning homes only to be trapped or buried in the street by falling buildings.

Aeneas, like the other brave men of Troy, left his home to help fight the invading Greeks. Eventually he made his way to the royal palace, hoping that this last stronghold could be defended. But there, too, the enemy had battered a way through. King Priam with his wife Hecuba and their daughters had taken refuge before the family altar when the Greek warriors rushed in. The old King's end came quickly, and seeing it, Aeneas suddenly remembered his own father, an old man like the King. Aeneas had been so anxious to defend his city that he had left his father, his wife and his young son alone and unprotected. The thought of what might have happened to them sickened him. Now his only concern was to return home.

He was struggling back through the dust and smoke that filled the doomed palace when he caught sight of a woman crouching in the shadows. She looked up in fear as he approached and he realized that he was looking at the beautiful Helen.
'This woman has been the cause of all our suffering,' he thought. 'It is she who has brought ruin to this once fair city and its people.'

In his sudden fury he took a firm grip on his sword and resolved to avenge the wrongs by killing her, there where she crouched. Before he could put his thoughts into action, however, he was aware that his mother, Venus, was beside him. She looked radiant and spoke with firm gentleness.
'Son, nothing will be gained by this act of blind fury. The woman is not to blame for what has happened, nor is Paris. Don't you see that it is the merciless gods who are destroying the splendour and power of this kingdom? You must flee, for your future lies beyond this shore. I have watched over those you left at home, keeping them safe until your return. Now go quickly. I shall protect you.'

With these words she vanished, but he felt the goddess guiding him through all the dangers he met on his way back home. So far his house had withstood the attacks of wandering bands of Greek soldiers, and although fires raged in many of the buildings round about, his home was untouched. Aeneas called to his family to prepare quickly for their escape. His old father Anchises said that he was too weak to leave and anyway he wanted to stay and meet the same fate as Troy. The pleadings of Aeneas and the other members of his household were of no avail.

Then several astounding things happened. To everyone's surprise the head of Ascanius, Aeneas' young son, was suddenly surrounded by a strange light and bright flames danced harmlessly through his hair. Anchises saw this as a divine omen and prayed to Jupiter, asking for a further sign to confirm the will of the gods. No sooner had he offered his prayer than a crash of thunder ripped through the air and a brilliant shooting star streaked low across the night sky, lighting up the whole city.

Anchises rose at once to leave. 'Gods of our race,' he cried, 'where you lead I shall follow.'

Everyone made their final preparations. Before leaving his home for the last time, Anchises carefully gathered up the statues from the household shrine and wrapped them in a bundle ready to take with him. These images of the family gods would ensure their good fortune on the journey ahead and bestow blessings on their new home. Since old Anchises was too infirm to walk, Aeneas carried him on his shoulders. Protected by the loving hand of Venus, the group made their way towards the nearest city gate. Aeneas kept Ascanius close beside him, holding his hand, while Creusa, his wife, walked just a few paces behind.

It was not until they had reached the safety of the countryside beyond the city wall that Aeneas realized the terrible truth: Creusa was no longer with them. Leaving the others safely hidden he returned to Troy, desperately searching for his beloved wife.

He retraced his steps through the smouldering remains of the city, repeating her name at every turn, until the streets rang with his cries. He was just giving up hope of ever finding her when she was suddenly before him. Instead of feeling joy at the sight of her he was gripped by fear, for it was not the real Creusa, but her ghost. 'Dear husband,' she said softly, 'do not grieve. The gods have ruled that I stay here. You must leave this place and cross the vast ocean to begin a new life in the Western Land. There beside the Tiber you will find happiness, a kingdom and a fair queen. Take care of our son, I beg you, and now—goodbye.'

Aeneas tried to grasp his wife, but his hands passed through her shadowy shape and she disappeared from his sight. He was left standing alone and bewildered in the deserted street.

When he returned to his friends and family he found a great crowd of people with them, a pathetic group of homeless refugees, waiting for him to lead them to exile beyond the sea. In the first light of dawn Aeneas lifted his father once more onto his shoulders, and with his new followers behind him he left Troy for ever and trudged towards the distant mountains.

Others, too, were leaving Troy for the last time. The Greeks, with their slaves and their stolen treasure, sailed for home. Those Trojans who, like Aeneas, had escaped death, crowded the roads leading away from the city. The war that had raged for ten years had ended in one fateful night.

Aeneas with his band of exiled survivors travelled overland to the Phrygian coast, south of Troy, and there began the task of building a fleet of ships. Then, sadly they set sail, with little idea of what was in store for them.

The first land they came to was Thrace. This country had been an ally of Troy in her more prosperous days, but the Trojan fugitives were not welcomed there so they decided to put their trust in the ocean once again. The winds and currents bore them south to the holy island of Delos, birthplace of the god Apollo. Here they were received well by the King and his people. Aeneas approached the sacred temple of Apollo to offer a heartfelt prayer, asking for guidance and reassurance.

Almost at once the god replied. The earth shook violently and a voice came from the depths below the temple: 'Long suffering Trojans, you must return to the land of your ancestors. From there the descendants of Aeneas shall rule the whole world.'

The oracle had spoken but the meaning of the words was unclear. Where was the land of their ancestors? Anchises knew the early traditions of Troy and spoke to the people with confidence: 'I am sure that Crete is the cradle of our race. It is an island owned by great Jupiter himself, a country of great cities and fertile plains. That's where we must go, with the help of the gods.'

He then made offerings at the altar before the temple, a bull each for Neptune and Apollo, a black sheep for Storm and a white sheep for the kindly west winds.

They boarded their ships once more and sped on south, threading their way among the many small islands of the Cyclades, all the winds and currents in their favour, until they reached the coast of Crete.

Once there they found a deserted part of the coast on which to settle, beached their ships and began work on building the walls of a new city. Everyone laboured with great enthusiasm and soon crops had been planted and homes established. Everything seemed to be going well until, as harvest time approached, the land was attacked by a strange disease. Many people were ill or died, the crops rotted in the fields, animals perished. No-one could understand what they had done to displease the gods.

One night, as Aeneas slept, the gods of Troy appeared to him in a dream. They told him that Crete was not the Trojans' final destination. The true home of the Trojan race was the Western Land, an ancient region called Hesperia or Italy. The gods said that he should urge his people on again, for their voyage must continue.

Inspired by this divine message the people quickly left Crete and sailed on in search of those far-off shores. As soon as they were out of sight of land, however, a sudden storm blew up. The fleet quickly became scattered and for three days and nights the ships were battered by winds and heavy seas. Jagged rocks along a nameless coast were another hazard, threatening to wreck the ships as they passed. Eventually the wind dropped and, using the oars, the travellers managed to bring the fleet to a safe harbour. Only later did they realize that the land they had

reached was the Strophades, home of the dreaded Harpies. These grim monsters had the bodies, wings and talons of ferocious birds but the heads and faces of women.

Weak with hunger after so many storm-tossed days at sea, the Trojans attacked and killed some of the cattle they found grazing unprotected on the meadows by the shore. They cooked the meat on fires along the curving beach and prepared for a feast. The smell of cooking soon attracted the Harpies and the air was suddenly full of the sounds of flapping wings and terrifying screams as the monsters swooped down, their hideous claws snatching up the food. The stench they left behind them was foul and everything they had touched was filthy.

The same thing happened on the following day, but by the third day the men had their weapons ready and attacked the birds as they swooped. The Harpies still snatched at the food, unharmed by the sword thrusts, and flew off screaming ferociously. Their leader, Calaeno, perched on a rock nearby and spoke a parting prophecy:

'How dare you come to our island, raiding our cattle and attacking us with your swords! For this wrong you shall be punished. Yes, you will finally come to Italy, that is your destiny, but you shall not make your home there until a terrible hunger has forced you to eat your own tables.'

She disappeared then, leaving the people feeling very despondent. It seemed that there would be no end to their troubles. Anchises and Aeneas decided to leave the island at once. They offered suitable prayers to the gods, asking for defence against danger on the voyage ahead. The ships were made ready once again and as the sails were unfurled, a favourable south wind blew them on their way.

Soon other islands came into view as the fleet sailed north along the coast of Greece, skirting the shores of Epirus until eventually it entered the harbour below the hill-city of Buthrotum. Here the Trojans were surprised and delighted, for this Greek kingdom was ruled by one of Priam's sons, Helenus. Their welcome was a splendid one and everyone rejoiced greatly at the happy meeting.

The days passed pleasantly but Aeneas knew that this was not their final destination and he was soon anxious to continue the voyage. He knew also that Helenus had prophetic powers and found an opportunity to question him about the future. As priest of Apollo, Helenus sacrificed bullocks before the altar of the god and said the formal prayers. Then, seized by the divine power, he was inspired to prophesy. 'Son of the goddess,' he said, addressing Aeneas, 'your destiny is sealed. You still have a long voyage ahead of you and many dangers await your ships. Eventually you will arrive on a far Italian shore and build there a great city.'

He went on to describe the details of the voyage to come, the places where it would be unwise to land and the course to steer around the twin dangers of Scylla and Charybdis, a six-headed monster and a dangerous whirlpool which lay in their path. He also foretold Aeneas' meeting with a mysterious prophetess, the Sibyl. 'I can tell you no more,' he said finally. 'Go then, and bring glory to Troy by your deeds.'

Helenus gave orders for a generous store of gifts to be put aboard the Trojan ships, including treasures of silver and gold. He gave them new weapons, too, and extra sailors to man the oars. After many farewells the fleet set forth. Once out to sea, Anchises stood on the quarter-deck of the leading ship and raised his voice in prayer: 'Gods of the earth and of the sea, give us a fair wind to help our voyage.'

As if in answer to his prayer, the breeze strengthened and the ships sped onward until they approached the coast of Sicily. There they sailed close to the thundering mountain of Etna, its volcanic mass belching smoke and showers of sparks. Soon afterwards the wind dropped suddenly and the fleet drifted gently towards the coast of the Cyclopes. This was an inhospitable land, peopled by a tribe of hideous one-eyed giants. As soon as they saw strangers approaching, the giants ran to the rocky shore, shouting and throwing huge stones to destroy the ships. Fortunately for Aeneas and his companions, the wind freshened again and they were able to make a hasty escape.

Without thinking of where they were going, the fleet headed towards the narrow strip of water between the whirlpool Charybdis and the rocks where the six-headed monster, Scylla, lived. Just in time they remembered Helenus' warning. The sails were trimmed and everyone pulled on the oars, desperate to save themselves from certain destruction. On one side of the channel the waters of the whirlpool swirled and boiled, threatening to suck whole ships down to the depths of the sea; on the other crouched the six-headed monster, waiting to snatch the crewmen from their oars, powerful enough to snap a mast with one blow from its ugly paw. With the strength of men fighting for their lives they managed to steer away from the danger, into calmer waters.

Again a kindly wind helped them on, blowing them round Sicily's southern shore until they reached Drepanum, a city which stood near a mountain called Eryx. There, perched high on the mountain, above the sea, was a fine temple dedicated to the worship of Venus. It was there, close to the shrine of his divine wife, that Anchises died. Perhaps the time and the place of his death were chosen by Venus? No-one knows.

Aeneas was left feeling close to despair. Anchises had been the best of fathers to him. The two men had shared the burden of leadership and now, so close to the end of their journey, death had come between them.

With the funeral rites over and the ashes of Anchises buried beneath a great mound of earth not far from Drepanum, the fleet set sail again, heading out to sea on what the Trojans believed was the last stage of their voyage.

Dido and Aeneas

The sea was calm as the Trojans set out from Drepanum, so the crews used their bronze-plated oars to speed the ships on their way. Just as they were out of sight of land a breeze sprang up and the sails were hoisted. The voyage was going well and all those aboard the ships felt a new surge of hope, thinking that their long journey would soon be over.

However, the goddess Juno, Queen of Heaven, was furious when she realized that the Trojans were at last nearing their destination. She had wanted to see Troy and the Trojans utterly destroyed and had fought on the side of her beloved Greeks to bring it about. She had always been jealous of the Trojan race and had tried repeatedly to stop Aeneas and his brave followers from reaching the Italian shore. It was she who had caused them to wander the seas, making them suffer so many hardships along the way.

The goddess, it was said, loved one city in the world above all others, and she was determined to make it the most powerful. That city was Carthage, situated on the Mediterranean coast of Africa, not far from Sicily, and inhabited by Phoenicians from distant Tyre. With Juno's help it had grown rich and powerful, and had conquered all the territory round about. Imagine her anger, then, when she learned that the plan of the Fates was to make the descendants of Aeneas masters of the world, masters even of the city she loved above all others.

'Am I not Queen?' she said to herself. 'Can I not defy the Fates and destroy the Trojan clan now, before they reach the Italian shore?'

Determined to protect her favourite city, she went straight to Aeolus, the King of the Winds. It was he who kept the roaring hurricanes locked safely away in a vast, dark cave under a mountain. From his throne on the mountain-top Aeolus ruled the winds, keeping the earth, the sea and the skies safe from their wild, destructive fury.

'Lord Aeolus,' said Juno quietly, 'will you grant one small favour?'

'Divine Queen,' replied Aeolus, 'just state your wish. I shall obey you without prompting. For it is to you and your husband Jupiter that I owe my powers.'

'Then this is my command. Sink the Trojan fleet which now sails between Sicily and Italy. Release your most ferocious winds and send them to stir up the sea, to batter their ships, and drown all those aboard.'

Immediately Aeolus struck a hole in the cliff wall of his mountain kingdom. The pent-up winds rushed out and together swept towards the sea in mad confusion. Clouds covered the sky, lightning flashed and flared, thunder crashed. The Trojans were terrified. The howling winds suddenly threw mountainous waves high into the air while sea and wind together smashed into the frail ships, tearing away sails, snapping spars and oars, ripping off bows and rudders. Some of the fleet were sent careering onto the jagged teeth of large rocks while others were sucked into great whirlpools and dragged deep below the surface. The sea was littered with wreckage and with items of cargo. Precious possessions salvaged from Troy or collected on the voyage were lost, and with them many of the valiant Trojan crewmen.

Neptune, god of the sea, soon realized what was happening and angrily came to the rescue. He saw the Trojan fleet being battered by the elements and guessed that Juno was to blame. Immediately he calmed the waves and commanded the winds to return to Aeolus with a message for their lord.
'I am sovereign of the ocean and not he. How dare he release you from your prison without my leave!'

Once more mighty Neptune looked out over his realm and saw the sea lying calm under a clear, untroubled sky. He saw, too, the remnants of the Trojan fleet, just seven ships, making for a sheltered cove on the African coast. Satisfied with what he saw he sank down once more to his underwater kingdom.

The ships were made fast and the weary sailors flung themselves thankfully onto the beach. Later, while everyone was busy preparing a meal from their meagre provisions, Aeneas climbed the hillside and looked out to the far horizon. The sea was empty. No more of his ships were afloat. Then, as he prepared to return to his companions, he looked down into a green valley below him and saw a herd of deer quietly grazing. Taking his bow and arrows he moved

nearer and quickly shot and killed seven of the deer, one for each of the surviving crews.

A feast was prepared and the company ate heartily. They also drank long draughts of wine from casks stored away in the ships' holds. After the meal Aeneas spoke words of comfort to his people and they all mourned the loss of their brave comrades.

From his place high in the heavens Jupiter looked down on the world below, and particularly on the stranded Trojans, camped on the shore not far from royal Carthage. He seemed lost in thought when Venus spoke to him. 'I am saddened by what has happened to my dear son Aeneas and to his faithful followers,' she said, her face wet with tears. 'Please tell me how they have offended you. Why are you making it impossible for them to reach Italy? And what about your promise to make my son's descendants great leaders of men? Is it, Father, that your will has changed?'

Great Jupiter looked kindly at his daughter and smiled before he replied.
'Do not be afraid,' he said at last, 'for all my promises will come true. Aeneas will build his city in Italy, and he will wage war and conquer many peoples. His fate is fixed, and so is that of his son Ascanius, who from now on will have a second name, Iulus. This Iulus shall be king for many years and shall establish a new city called Alba Longa. There kings shall reign for three hundred years, until a royal priestess shall give birth to twin sons. Mars shall be their father and one of the twins, Romulus by name, will build a strong city, calling his people Romans after himself. These Romans will be masters of the world. This is my promise.'

As soon as he had finished speaking, Jupiter sent Mercury, the messenger of the gods, to Dido, Queen of Carthage, ordering her to welcome the Trojans as honoured guests and not to regard them as enemies.

Meanwhile, Aeneas, restless as ever, was anxious to discover where he had landed and who the inhabitants of the country were. He left his men guarding the ships and ventured out in the first light of dawn, taking just one companion, Achates. His son Ascanius stayed behind on the shore.

Venus, disguised as a lovely young huntress, met them as they went. They talked together and in the conversation the goddess told Aeneas about the country they were in, about the people who had settled there and about Queen Dido. It was only when she was leaving them that Aeneas at last recognized his mother, but before he could speak she had vanished. Invisible, she watched them as they walked on and, fearing for their safety, covered them in a magic mist. Protected in this way they walked unseen towards the city, passing through the bustling crowds that swarmed everywhere. The people were all intent on building and the two Trojans stopped to stare at the activity all around them.

They walked on to the very heart of the city, where the people were building a great temple in honour of their goddess Juno. Again they stood astonished, gazing at the size and richness of the building and at its skilfully worked decoration which showed events from the history of their own city of Troy. They were so entranced by this that they failed to notice the approach of the beautiful Queen herself.

Accompanied by armed guards and countless young attendants, Dido entered the temple and sat on a high throne at its centre. At once she began the task of announcing new laws and making wise judgements. As this was happening Aeneas noticed a large crowd approaching. Everyone seemed very excited and Aeneas and Achates, still invisible, were amazed for there at the head of the crowd were several of their own countrymen, men they had thought drowned in the storm only the day before. They were overjoyed to see them but also uneasy because the circumstances were so mysterious.

They listened carefully as the Trojans addressed the Queen, telling her of their hopes and fears then appealing to her for mercy and for the means to repair their damaged ships.

Dido replied generously. 'Trojans,' she began, 'everyone has heard of your brave city and its dreadful end. You are welcome to stay as long as you wish. I shall give you whatever you need to make your ships safe for your voyage to Italy. But what about your leader, Aeneas? Perhaps the storm drove him to shore nearby. I shall send men along the coast to search for him.'

Hearing this, Aeneas wondered what he should do, but Venus took the decision out of his hands: the cloud of invisibility with which she had surrounded him suddenly evaporated and, to everyone's surprise, he stepped forward, his face and eyes shining with a divine light. 'I am Aeneas,' he announced. 'May the gods reward you, gracious Dido, for your mercy and generosity.'

The sight of Aeneas moved Dido greatly for she knew that before her stood no ordinary mortal but the son of a goddess, a man destined for future greatness. Immediately she invited them all to her palace, giving orders for a royal banquet to be prepared in honour of her guests. Aeneas could not relax. He worried about the safety of his son Ascanius and finally he sent Achates to fetch the boy. He also gave orders for rich gifts fit for a queen to be brought from the ships.

Meanwhile, Venus was planning a way to safeguard her son. She feared the power of Juno, suspecting that she was planning to trap Aeneas

by some trick and that she would not hesitate to use Dido in her scheme. Quickly deciding what to do, she enlisted the help of another of her sons, Cupid, the god of love. Cupid disguised himself as Ascanius, took the boy's place and went with Achates to Carthage. Venus sent the real Ascanius into a deep and delightful sleep, then carried him by her magic powers to a secret, far-away hiding-place, until Cupid's errand was completed.

By the time Achates and the young god arrived at the palace with their gifts, a magnificent meal had been made ready. The Trojans, the Queen and all the nobles of Carthage took their places at the tables and the banquet began. Dido was very impressed by the gifts placed before her, but what distracted her most was the boy she took to be Ascanius. She could not stop gazing at him. When the boy had lovingly greeted his father he approached the Queen and stayed close beside her for the rest of the evening. Poor Dido did not realize that Cupid already had her in his power for, following the orders of Venus, he was gently filling the Queen's heart and mind with feelings of love.

The banquet proceeded and when everyone had eaten, the drinking-bowls were refilled. After offering libations to the gods everyone relaxed and enjoyed the songs of Iopas, a talented entertainer. The drinking and talking lasted well into the night. Then Dido called for silence and invited Aeneas to speak to the company.
'Come, brave Aeneas,' she said, 'we have only heard parts of your story of adventure. Now tell us the whole tale from the beginning.'

So Aeneas spoke and everyone present listened intently as he told of the Greeks' trick and of the end of Troy, of his escape with his fellow countrymen and of their wanderings in search of a new home. Dawn was just breaking when the Trojan leader came to the end of his tale and the weary listeners fell asleep where they sat. Dido, however, could not sleep. She was troubled by the events of the previous day and the moving story which Aeneas had told. She could think of nothing but the Trojan stranger. Her husband had been killed tragically by her

brother many years before and since then no man had stirred even the slightest interest in her. Now, in spite of her common sense and high resolve, she found herself falling in love.

Later she confided in her sister and together they visited the holy shrines to pray and offer sacrifices. None of this seemed to help poor Dido; she felt utterly miserable. She found excuses to be alone with Aeneas but even then was afraid to tell him what she really felt. She wandered about the city lost in dreams and no longer took any interest in the affairs of state. Without their Queen to guide and inspire them the people soon stopped work. The building of her noble city, with its high towers and battlemented walls, came to a standstill. Such was the power of love!

Juno and Venus, of course, took great interest in what was happening. Neither trusted the other, but together they decided on a plan. They agreed to use their powers to bring Dido and Aeneas closer together while the pair were out hunting on the following day.

Very early in the morning the two hunting parties assembled. Dido, riding a splendid horse, was dressed in purple and gold and had with her a large company of nobles and attendants. Seeing Aeneas at the head of the Trojan party Dido was once more astounded by his handsome looks. To her he had the grace and beauty of Apollo himself.

They travelled a long way from Carthage, to places in the hills where wild animals roamed. The hunting went well until, later in the day, a violent storm arose, as if from nowhere, as Juno blackened the sky and sent down torrents of rain and hail. The hunters scattered and, as the goddesses had agreed, Dido and Aeneas chose the same cave in which to shelter. It was as if all the powers in nature were combining to unite the royal pair and Venus, goddess of love, and Juno, mistress of marriage, looked on as Dido and Aeneas, both filled with love's passion, fell into each other's arms.

When they returned to Carthage everyone realized at once what had happened. Dido was even heard to use the word 'marriage' to describe the partnership. Hard fact and sordid rumour soon spread through all the cities of Africa.

Eventually the story reached King Iarbus, the ruler of a neighbouring territory. He claimed to be a son of Jupiter and an African nymph and had for a long time been trying to persuade Dido to marry him. Now, furious at her choice, he made a direct appeal to his father before the altar in Jupiter's sacred temple.

'Great Jupiter, have my prayers and offerings all been in vain? How can Queen Dido refuse so often to marry me and then take this vagrant Aeneas as her lord?'

His prayer was heard. Jupiter took careful note of what was happening in Carthage then sent Mercury with a stern message for Aeneas. Obediently Mercury put on his golden, winged sandals, took up his wand and left Olympus, travelling at the winds' speed. Aeneas was directing the building of new houses when Mercury appeared and delivered his divine warning.

'Shame on you Aeneas! Have you forgotten your destiny and the destiny of your son? Italy awaits your arrival. Do not linger here a moment longer.'

Mercury vanished as swiftly as he had appeared, leaving Aeneas speechless and afraid. He knew that he must leave Carthage at once but what would the Queen do and say? While he was trying to think of a tactful way to break the news to Dido, he gave orders for the fleet to be made seaworthy immediately. The Trojans were delighted to be continuing their journey and they set to work at once, repairing and painting the ships, checking the sails and oars for damage and collecting stores for the voyage. All this activity could not be hidden from Dido for long and when she realized what was happening she completely lost control, running wildly around the city, screaming and shouting.

'You traitor,' she screamed at Aeneas. 'How dare you forsake me. Is the love we share nothing to you? You're mad to put to sea in the depths of winter. And what about me? Am I to be left alone and unprotected?'

Aeneas tried in vain to console her but although it was very painful for him he had to tell her that he must leave.

'This is not my own choice,' he explained, 'the gods, even Jupiter himself, direct me to voyage on to Italy.'

It was as if Dido's love turned from that moment to pure hate. She would not be comforted and nothing Aeneas said could make her see reason. Speechless with rage, she stormed out of the room. Aeneas obeyed the divine command with a miserable heart and returned to continue preparing his fleet for the sea.

Watching the bustle of activity on the beach below her palace, Dido knew now that Aeneas would go; nothing she did or said would stop him. In her madness and grief she resolved to die and, ordering a great funeral pyre to be built, she placed on it all the things from the palace which belonged to Aeneas.

'All this will burn, yes, even our bridal bed, on the day he departs,' she ordered.

On the night before Aeneas planned to sail, when the ships were drawn up ready on the beach and the stores all safely loaded aboard, Aeneas fell into an exhausted sleep. Almost at once Mercury appeared to him with a warning to hurry away while he still had the chance. He awoke suddenly, found that a favourable wind was blowing, and ordered the ships to leave immediately.

In the first light of dawn Dido looked out and saw the Trojan fleet disappearing towards the north. At first she thought of sending ships to pursue them but the Trojans had too good a start and she knew that her own fleet would never catch them now. Instead, she cursed Aeneas and all his descendants, calling on the divine powers to avenge her betrayal. In her madness she scrambled to the top of the pyre, unsheathed a sword and, with a final despairing prayer, fell forward onto the blade. Dido's sister was the first to reach her. In vain she tried to revive the dying Queen, holding her gently and whispering words of comfort through her tears. At last Juno took pity and sent her messenger Iris, goddess of the rainbow, to release Dido's spirit from the earthly world.

As news of the death of the Queen spread through the city, the priests led her mourning people to the pyre and solemnly lit a funeral fire beneath it. Flames leaped into the air and a column of thick smoke rose slowly upwards while, far out at sea, the Trojan fleet disappeared over the horizon.

Adventures in Sicily

From far out to sea Aeneas and his men looked back towards
Carthage and saw the great pall of smoke hanging above the city.
Below the smoke they could just make out the bright flames of a fire.
Secretly guessing what it might be, the men muttered uneasily to one
another, avoiding Aeneas' eyes. Wrapped in his cloak, Aeneas
himself stood in the stern of his ship, staring back to Carthage until
nothing but sea and sky could be seen.

 As they sailed on, a large, gloomy bank of clouds appeared and the
wind began to blow harder. Palinurus, the helmsman on Aeneas'
ship, looked up and said, 'We shall never make Italy if this weather
holds. The wind is dead against us. But if we change course now it
will drive us to the safe harbours of Sicily's coast.'
'Change course, then, Palinurus,' said Aeneas. 'Steer with the wind.
We will trust to Fortune.'

 With a following wind the fleet raced across the water and, to
everyone's satisfaction, landed on a familiar shore. It was Drepanum,
the place where they had buried the ashes of Aeneas' father,
Anchises, just a year before. The land was inhabited by Trojans, like
themselves, and ruled by Acestes, son of a Trojan woman and
Crimisus the river god. The people greeted the returned travellers
with great joy.

The next day, after they had rested, Aeneas called his followers together and announced that they were to celebrate the anniversary of his father's death.

'I'm quite sure,' he said, 'that the powers in heaven have brought us at this time to the very place where the ashes of Anchises lie buried. We must pay proper respect and celebrate in a way worthy of his memory.'

Then, following Aeneas' example, all the men placed wreaths of myrtle on their heads in honour of the occasion. He led everyone to the large burial mound and there poured sacred offerings of wine, milk and blood, calling upon the spirit of his noble father. As if in answer a huge and magnificently coloured snake slid out from under the shrine. It slithered all the way round the grave, then tasted each offering in turn before disappearing into its hole. Aeneas was greatly encouraged by this strange happening, which he interpreted as a good omen, and continued with the ritual. More animals were sacrificed and offerings were heaped on the altars.

A great feast followed and then, several days later, Aeneas announced the beginning of the funeral games. News of this spread far and wide and soon great crowds had assembled, everyone eager for entertainment. The games began with a regatta, the main event being a rowing race for four specially chosen ships of the fleet. Together the four vessels dashed forward out of the harbour, the oars churning the water to foam, then out to sea for a short distance to round a group of half-submerged rocks before returning to the starting point. The event caused great excitement especially as one ship nearly capsized at the rocky turn.

Next the people assembled in a natural amphitheatre nearby for the running events. These attracted a great number of competitors, all eager to win a fine prize and the victor's olive wreath. With the races over and the young athletes properly rewarded, Aeneas called for competitors for the boxing. Only two men fought for the prize, both heavyweight champions and both desperate to win. In the end Aeneas had to stop the fight when it became obvious that one man would kill the other by his ferocious punches.

After the boxing came an archery contest. Several heats were held and four archers tied in equal first place; the crowd settled in silence to watch the final. A ship's mast had been set up with a dove tied by a cord to the top. The first man's arrow only struck the mast, the second archer cut the cord with his arrow, while the third skilfully caught the bird in flight and brought it to the ground. That left the fourth man, Acestes. To the surprise of the spectators, he simply loosed his arrow into the sky instead of taking careful aim. Even more surprising was the fact that the flying arrow caught fire and fell impressively in a blazing arc, surely a sign from the gods.

The final event was for the Trojan boys and they put on an impressive riding display, parading round the arena cheered by the crowd. Young Ascanius was there, leading his own formation of riders, mounted on a horse that Dido had given him. After the parade the young horsemen performed a mock battle, surprising everyone with their skill.

Juno still resented the good fortune being enjoyed by the exiled Trojans and once more she planned to delay them. She sent her special messenger Iris swiftly to earth on an errand of mischief. On the beach Iris found a group of Trojan woman weeping and complaining together. They were grieving for Anchises but also for their own plight for they were weary of the endless voyaging and still without a proper home. Quickly Iris disguised herself as an old woman and joined the group. She encouraged them in their complaining, saying that they should give up any hope of reaching Italy and settle there, where they were. With that she snatched up a burning torch from the nearby shrine of Neptune and ran towards the Trojan fleet drawn up on the beach crying, 'Help me to burn the ships which bring us ill fortune.'

The women were seized by a sudden madness, and following the example of the goddess, quickly set fire to every ship.

When the people at the games saw the clouds of black smoke rising from the shore they shouted to raise the alarm. With great presence of mind, Ascanius rode off towards the beach, followed by the rest of the Trojan boys. He saw

at a glance what had happened and shouted to the women to stop. His shout broke Juno's spell and they ran in all directions looking for hiding places. By the time Aeneas and the other spectators arrived, the flames were roaring through the ships, completely out of control.

Aeneas was desperate. He prayed to Jupiter for help, believing that even then the fleet could be saved from destruction and almost before he had finished speaking rain began to pour down in torrents. The mighty storm that raged was so violent that the earth itself shook with Jupiter's thunder. The ships were flooded with rain and every fire was extinguished. Of all the ships in the fleet, only four were damaged beyond repair.

Although the ships were saved, this was yet another blow to Trojan hopes and Aeneas began to wonder whether after all he should give up hope of ever landing in Italy. Just then an old man called Nautes, who was known as a person who could see into the future, came up to him. 'Son of the goddess,' he began, 'I have read the signs and humbly advise you. Speak to noble Acestes, your kinsman, and make plans

together. There are many of us who are worn out by travel or too old and frail to suffer any more hardship. Leave us here to make a new home for ourselves. Build us a city and call it Acesta in honour of the King.'

Aeneas thought about this plan and worried over it for a long time, unable to make up his mind what to do. Then one night his father appeared to him in a vision with a message from Jupiter.

'My son, Troy's destiny is a heavy burden for you, but great Jupiter watches over you. Remember how he answered your prayer and quenched the fire in your ships. The advice of old Nautes is sound, so do as he suggests. Choose the best and most resilient of your people to venture on with you to Italy, to the land of Latium. Once there you will have a long, hard struggle to establish yourselves. Day approaches so I must go, but one thing more. Before you arrive in Latium you will be led by the holy Sibyl to the land of Death where I shall meet you again and tell you more about your future home and the destiny of our race.'

With these words the spirit of Anchises disappeared. Aeneas reverently prayed to the spirit of Troy and to Vesta and made suitable offerings. Then he roused Acestes and also his closest companions and told them what had happened. No time was lost in putting ideas into action and work went ahead immediately on building the new Trojan city for those who were to stay behind. The fire damage to the ships was soon repaired and the fleet was once more ready for sea.

When all the preparations were complete the people made offerings to the gods, then feasted for nine days. By the end of that time a favourable south wind had begun to blow and Aeneas could delay no longer. A crowd gathered on the shore to say goodbye to the travellers. In the sadness of parting those who had chosen to stay in Sicily now wished to sail with Aeneas— but the decision had been taken and could not now be changed. Aeneas stood high on the stern of his ship to address them.

'Good people, our destiny is in the hands of the gods. Latium lies ahead for some of us, and a hard struggle, too. The rest of you have suffered enough and I entrust you to Acestes. Live happily under his rule in our new Trojan city. Now wish us well.'

He then ordered the sacrifice of three bullocks and a lamb on the shore as the ships moved gently towards the open sea. Wearing a wreath of olive leaves he made his own offering of meat and wine, throwing both into the water. As if in reply, the wind freshened, driving the fleet forward on its journey north into the unknown.

Now that the Trojan fleet was once more at sea and open to another of Juno's spiteful attacks, Venus began to worry. In desperation she went to Neptune, asking him to ensure a safe voyage for her son and his companions. Neptune was very sympathetic. 'Do not be afraid,' he said, 'for Aeneas will reach the harbour at Cumae in Italy safely. Only one more Trojan will be lost on the voyage, and his life will only be taken for the safety of the rest.'

Then, mounting his chariot and giving his horses full rein, the sea god sped away over the surface of the waves, calming the ocean and dispersing the storm clouds as he passed.

Sailing conditions were now perfect for the Trojan fleet and it ran happily before the wind. Aeneas' ship, under the command of Palinurus, led the rest. During the night, when the crews were asleep, Somnus the sleep god visited Palinurus as he stood at the helm, tempting him to rest for a while and leave the ship to steer itself. Palinurus glanced at the sky and at the gentle sea. All seemed well—but he was too experienced a sailor to trust even a calm sea and a clear sky. He remained watchful at his post but as he stared up at the billowing sails and at the stars beyond, Somnus waved a magic branch of sleep over him and, still grasping the helm firmly, Palinurus dozed. As soon as Somnus saw his eyes closing, he toppled him over the stern into the sea. Carrying the helm with him, Palinurus sank into the dark waters.

With Neptune's help, the ship sailed safely on its course and it was only when Aeneas awoke to feel the ship wallowing badly that he discovered the loss of his helmsman. Palinurus was not only a fine sailor but also an old and trusted friend, a man who had survived so many of the sea's dangers at Aeneas' side. Aeneas wept as he guided the ship on through the night.

The golden bough

At last the Trojan fleet sailed within sight of land and reached the Italian coast at Cumae. After years of adventure and hardship the Trojans had arrived in the country of their hopes and dreams. The ships were anchored and the people went ashore, eager and excited, to set about the task of making camp.

Aeneas and Achates made their way inland, climbing a nearby hill to survey the countryside. On the hill they found a shrine to the god Apollo and a sacred grove dedicated to Diana. According to legend this temple had been built by an architect named Daedalus. Long ago he had been commissioned by the king of Crete to build a maze, the Labyrinth, as a prison for a monster called the Minotaur. Helped by Daedalus, the Greek hero Theseus killed the monster and to punish Daedalus for his part in the adventure, the King locked the architect and his son Icarus inside the Labyrinth. Daedalus, however, was a great inventor. He managed to construct two pairs of wings and he and Icarus flew from their prison and out over the sea towards Italy. Icarus did not complete the journey. In his pride he flew too near the sun and the wax that held the wings to his body melted, plunging him to his death in the sea below. Daedalus flew on to land safely at Cumae. The temple he built there was decorated with sculptures showing the whole story of Theseus and the Minotaur and Aeneas was so fascinated by the scenes that he failed to notice someone approaching across the grass. It was the priestess of Apollo and Diana, the Sibyl who, inspired by Apollo, spoke his prophecies and interpreted his messages to human beings.
'You should not be standing here looking at pictures, Trojan Aeneas,' she said angrily. 'There are rites to be performed. The gods must be honoured. Come with me.'

The two men followed her to a cavern in the hillside, a cavern with a hundred openings. It was from these that the Sibyl called her answers to those who asked about their futures. As they came to the cave's entrance, she cried out in sudden ecstacy: 'Apollo is here, I feel him. Pray now. Ask your fate.'

Her appearance had suddenly altered; she was pale, her long hair flew out from her head, she trembled and heaved. The Trojans were afraid. Then Aeneas summoned his courage and uttered a prayer to the god. 'Lord Apollo, may Troy's bad fortune end here. Let us, the remnant of Troy, be spared, if it is your divine will. Grant us a home in this land and the kingdom we are destined to inherit.'

Inside the cave the Sibyl again shook and struggled as the god possessed her, forcing her to speak his will. From the hundred openings came the wild booming sounds of her voice. 'Your adventures at sea are over. You shall be powerful in Lavinium, but before that the wars you must fight will be terrible ones. Even the river Tiber will run with blood. The odds against you will seem heavy but do not give up the struggle. Help will come from an unexpected source—from a Greek city.'

After that she spoke in strange riddles which they did not understand. Finally she became silent. Then Aeneas asked how he could enter the world of the dead, for he had heard that the entrance to it was close by.

'I long to see my father,' he said, 'and to speak with him face to face. You have some influence with Hecate, the dark goddess. Surely you can show me the way. Others have gone there before now and returned.'

Again the Sibyl's voice echoed from the cave. 'Son of the Goddess, be warned. The way in is easy, for the gates of that kingdom are always open. Returning to the daylight world is the difficult part and few have ever achieved it. However, if your heart is set on this scheme I will tell you what to do.'

Aeneas listened eagerly while the priestess told him about a golden bough hidden deep in the forest. 'Anyone entering the world below must take the bough as a gift for Proserpine, Queen of that dark realm. Each time the bough is plucked a new one grows in its place but only if the Fates allow it can the bough be pulled free. Before you go to find it, you must arrange the funeral of one of your comrades who is lying dead upon the shore. Go now.'

Aeneas and Achates walked sadly away, wondering what new disaster had occurred just when they thought they were safely established on land. On the beach they found the Trojans crowded round the body of a man named Misenus. Misenus had been better than anyone else at playing the bronze battle trumpet and according to eye-witnesses, he had been standing on the rocks blowing into a conch shell horn when some force had pushed him into the sea and drowned him. They thought that it must have been a jealous sea spirit who had punished him for trying to imitate the music of the gods.

Whatever had killed him, he now lay lifeless upon the sand. The only thing to do was to arrange a fitting funeral and, equipped with ropes and axes, the men hurried into the nearby forest to fetch wood for the funeral pyre. Aeneas, carrying his own sharp axe, went ahead, plunging deeper into the forest than the others, hoping to catch a glimpse of the golden bough. Just then two doves appeared and seemed to lead him on. He knew that doves were his mother's sacred birds and silently he called on her to help him in his search.

The doves flew onwards a little at a time and Aeneas kept them in sight until finally they flew up and settled high in the branches of a holm-oak. There, through the dark green leaves of the tree he saw a gleam of bright gold. It was the bough he was looking for. The breeze touched it and its metallic leaves tinkled softly. Aeneas reached forward and pulled the branch. It broke away easily and as he moved away another grew in its place, just as the Sibyl had foretold. Immediately he retraced his steps and took the sacred bough to the Sibyl's shrine.

By the time Aeneas returned to his people the pyre was nearly complete. The body of Misenus was lifted carefully to the top and draped with purple cloth. They duly completed the ceremonies and made their offerings, then set fire to the stacked-up timber. It burned fiercely for a long time then, when only ashes smouldered, the bones were placed in a bronze urn. The last words, the words of farewell, were spoken and the remains were buried under a mound of earth. Behind it towered the headland known from that day as Misenum in honour of the Trojan.

The next day, long before dawn, Aeneas returned to the Sybil, taking with him animals for the sacrifice that would be needed before he could undertake the strange journey to the Underworld. She led him to the mouth of a cave hidden in the depths of the forest and protected by the deep waters of a lake. This was Avernus, the entrance to the Underworld. From the opening came clouds of poisonous vapour and without divine help, no living thing could approach it safely. A stone altar stood there and the Sibyl ordered the sacrifice of four black bullocks, calling loudly to Hecate as their blood ran down. Hecate, the patron of witches and sorcerors, was also a powerful goddess of the Underworld and it was important to please her. Next Aeneas offered a black-fleeced lamb and a barren cow to the other deities of the Underworld. He was just finishing the ritual when the ground began to shake and rumble; in the distance he could clearly hear the sound of baying hounds. All nature stirred at the approach of Hecate and the Sibyl cried out loudly, 'Now brave Trojan, draw your sword and summon up all your courage. The time to act has come.'

With that she ran forward towards the gloomy entrance of the cave, Aeneas following close behind. They went first into a dark, lonely region of gloom inhabited by shadows. Here they saw all the things which bring pain to human life, everything ugly and misshapen. On one side were Grief and Care, Disease and Old Age, on the other Fear, Hunger, War and Agony. A large and aged tree with long, arm-like branches stood in the centre with the ghastly shapes of nightmares clinging beneath its leaves. It was at this place, too, that monsters had their lairs, writhing and hissing together. Aeneas trembled with fear and leaped forward in alarm to attack them with his sword, but the Sibyl warned him that they were without substance, just shadows.

A short distance further on they came to the seething, muddy waters that bordered the Underworld, the rivers of Grief and of Wailing, Acheron and Cocytus. There they met Charon guarding the river crossing, his flimsy boat tied to the bank nearby. The old man had a forbidding appearance. He was dressed in filthy rags, his beard and hair unkempt, his fierce eyes flaming bright. A great crowd of souls was moving back and forth along the river-side, all looking towards the opposite shore and begging

Charon to carry them across. Some the boatman accepted as passengers, others he pushed back, crossly. Aeneas was puzzled and asked his guide for an explanation.

'Charon the ferryman only takes those whose bones have received proper burial,' she said. 'These souls waiting helplessly here are the unburied dead and they must stay here for a hundred years before Charon can ferry them over.'

Aeneas stood and pondered, full of sorrow for those trapped, unhappy souls. Looking among them he saw some he knew, men of his own fleet drowned at sea and his old friend Palinurus, too, lurking in the shadows.

The Sibyl urged Aeneas on towards the river-side but the ferryman saw them coming and angrily shouted a challenge.

'Stay there. Come no closer but tell me what you want. Only ghosts are permitted to pass this way, so declare yourselves.'

The Sibyl answered him. 'Have no fear, for we intend no harm. This is Trojan Aeneas, a good man and valiant in battle. He comes only to visit his father who lives here with the blessed.'

Charon still looked fiercely at them, unmoved by the Sibyl's words. She then took the golden bough from beneath her robe and at once he led them to his craft. The flimsy vessel was unaccustomed to ferrying living beings and it creaked alarmingly as they went, while muddy water seeped in through the bottom. As they landed, the Sibyl gave Aeneas the golden bough.

Once across they faced a new and frightening hazard, the three-headed monster Cerberus. It crouched, barking, in a huge cavern and refused to let the travellers pass. The Sibyl was again prepared and threw the creature a drugged honey cake which it ate hungrily. The cake soon had its effect, for the monster slumped forward and slept, allowing them to pass by in safety.

Sounds of pathetic crying and wailing reached them as they went on. These were made by the ghosts of children and babies who had died suddenly. Next to them lodged the spirits of those condemned to death on a false charge, while further on were those who had hated life and killed themselves. Beyond, the travellers discovered the Fields of Mourning, a place of

myrtle groves, haunted by those who had been driven to death by the pains of love. It was here amongst the shadows that Aeneas saw the sad figure of someone he knew well, the sad queen who had loved him so passionately. All his feelings of tenderness for her returned and he spoke softly to her.

'Poor Dido, did I bring you to this? I did not leave you willingly, you must believe that. Heaven itself commanded me to go, just as it commands me now to travel through this dark pit. I swear this by all that is sacred. Please look at me and say that you understand.'

She would not look or speak; hatred still gripped her heart and she turned away and disappeared among the shadows. Aeneas wept, full of pity, and sorrowing at her terrible fate.

He and the Sibyl continued on their way, coming next to the place reserved for those who had fallen bravely in battle. There he saw the spirits of many he knew, the men who had fought beside him defending Troy. They crowded round him, pleased to see him, asking him a thousand questions. He would have lingered there with his old comrades had not the Sibyl hurried him on his way.

'Our time here is short,' she said, 'we must go on quickly. You see ahead that the road divides. Our way to Elysium, the Happy Place, is the one that passes beneath the walls of mighty Pluto's palace. The other road leads to Tartarus, the place where the wicked are punished.'

Even from where they stood they could hear loud groaning, the clanking of chains being dragged about and the cruel crack of a whip. Afraid but fascinated, Aeneas stood still, looking towards this place of misery and pain. It was strongly fortified with thick walls and had a massive gateway. Around it flowed the Phlegethon, a river of scorching flames full of white-hot rocks tumbled along by the current. Aeneas turned to his guide and said, 'Great priestess, tell me please what sort of kingdom this is. Who are those who go there to be punished so harshly?'

'I cannot show you what is beyond that gate, for no good person may enter there,' replied the Sibyl. 'When Hecate made me her priestess she explained about the punishments given to the wicked. It is here that Rhadamanthus judges all those who were wicked during their lives. He divides the guilty from the innocent and at once the terrible avenging Fury leaps onto the guilty ones, driving them forward with her whip and threatening them with the snakes in her left hand. Then the mighty doors grind slowly open. Inside waits the monstrous Hydra, its fifty heads writhing, each black mouth open. You cannot imagine the horror of the sight. Beyond is Tartarus itself, a dark pit of immense depth and a place of eternal torment for those who dared to challenge the authority of the gods or who broke their laws. Their punishments and their crimes are too many and too terrible to list.'

Hurrying on, they took the road that led away from Tartarus and towards their destination, the home of the blessed spirits. They approached the gateway, walking together through the shadows. At the entrance Aeneas sprinkled holy water over himself then took the golden bough and placed it reverently on the doorstep as an offering to the goddess Proserpine, Queen of the Underworld.

Then they entered the Happy Place, a bright, airy country of green meadows and shady woodland. The spirits who lived there enjoyed all their favourite pastimes from the world above. Aeneas stood watching the athletics and the wrestling, the dancing and singing. Orpheus was there playing his lyre for the dancers and there, too, were the heroes of old, his own ancestors. He saw Dardanus, the founder of Troy, together with many others, all taking pleasure in their horses, chariots and fine weapons just as they had done in life.

Aeneas and the Sibyl moved on to a grove of sweet-scented bay trees growing at the source of Eridanus, a river which flows on into the world of the living. Here were gathered those who had lived blamelessly and those who had given much to make the lives of others better. Seeing the newcomers, they gathered round and the Sibyl asked where Anchises could be found. The directions were easy to follow. They had to descend a steep hill into the country below, which gleamed in the heavenly light. There before them they saw Anchises standing thoughtfully in a grassy valley. Suddenly he

looked up to see Aeneas walking towards him. He was overjoyed and cried out through his tears, 'It's you at last. I knew that you would come, despite the hardships and dangers. Let me look at you and hear you speak to me.'

Aeneas' face, too, was wet with tears. He wanted to embrace his father, but that was impossible in the realm of spirits. Instead he looked at Anchises and said, 'It was you, appearing to me so often, who made me venture to this place. I had to come.'

Anchises was eager to show his son more of the land of happiness and led him to the banks of the river Lethe which gently flowed nearby. Along the banks swarmed a multitude of spirits. These, Anchises explained, were spirits fated to return to the living world who must first drink from this river of forgetfulness.
'The souls of all the dead must come here to the Underworld to be cleansed,' he explained. 'Eventually they are sent here to be prepared for their ascent back into the world of the living.'

Anchises led his son to a place where they could see the whole crowd of shadowy souls. 'Now I will show you what is to come,' announced Anchises, 'for here, amongst this throng, are the souls who will inherit our name. There is Silvius your last child, there Procas with Numitor, both Kings of Alba Longa, and there someone who will take after you, Silvius Aeneas. They are fine young men, you must agree. Now you must see someone else. There he is in his twin-plumed helmet. He is Romulus, a child of Mars. He shall start great Rome on its way to rule the whole earth. Now look at those people there, they are all your family.'

Aeneas stood, staring in astonishment as his father pointed out even more of his successors, and with them many of the leaders and heroes who would fashion the greatness of Rome. Among them was Augustus Caesar, the man destined to rule and extend the mighty Empire. As Aeneas watched the endless procession, his father foretold many of the events in the long history of Rome, inspiring Aeneas with hope for the future. Anchises also spoke of the troubled times Aeneas still had to face, giving him sound advice about the way to overcome each crisis.

All too soon, it seemed, the time came for them to depart. Still talking, Anchises led his son and the Sibyl to the ivory gate of sleep and sent them through it, back to the world of the living.

War in Italy

When Aeneas had thanked the Sibyl and left her in the woods above Cumae he made his way down to the harbour where his ships rode peacefully at anchor.

Once more the fleet set sail and the voyage continued north along the Italian coast, helped by a steady following wind. Neptune kept a watchful eye, guiding the ships to the place where the river Tiber flowed out into the sea. At this place of thick woods and yellow sandy beaches the Trojans went ashore, wondering whether at last this was to be their new home.

The people in that part of the country were called Latins or Laurentines. Their king was Latinus, an old man who had enjoyed a long and peaceful reign. He claimed descent from the god Saturn but his only son had been killed when still a boy. However, he did have a daughter, Lavinia, a girl who was wooed by many eligible young men from all over Italy. Among them was Turnus, King of the neighbouring Rutulians. He was by far the most handsome of the suitors and was the one favoured by the Queen, Amata. Lavinia would have married Turnus had not two strange happenings caused Latinus to hesitate. The first was the arrival of a swarm of bees which settled in a sacred laurel tree in the palace courtyard. The palace soothsayer saw this as a sign that strangers were coming to settle the land and make the city their stronghold. The second portent was much more dramatic: Lavinia's hair suddenly caught fire. Flames and sparks surrounded her head, forming a halo of light, but she remained unhurt. This was seen to mean two things; fame for the girl, but devastating war for the people.

The King consulted the local oracle and after he had made his offerings at the holy place Latinus heard the spirit voice. The message was clear: 'Do not marry your daughter to a man of the Italian race. Someone is coming from across the sea to be her husband and to make your nation, far in the future, greater than any other.'

Latinus was delighted and hurriedly explained the news to his people. They had already heard that a company of Trojans had landed on the banks of the Tiber, so they waited expectantly for the strangers to make contact with them.

Meanwhile the Trojans had set up camp near their ships and were

58

living very simply on their own stores and on whatever food the countryside provided. One day as they sat down to eat they piled fruit onto hard, flat cakes, not bothering with plates or tables. Having eaten the meagre fruit and still being hungry, they began to eat the hard cakes. Suddenly Ascanius cried jokingly, 'Look, we're eating the tables as well!' His words were greeted not by laughter but by a strange silence, for everyone there remembered the prophecy of the Harpy Calaeno: 'You shall not make your home in Italy until a terrible hunger has forced you to eat your own tables.' Then, suddenly, one of them began to laugh and in a moment they were all joining in, embracing one another with happiness. Their long voyage was over and here at last was their new home. They offered prayers and sacrifices to the gods and in answer, the thunder of Jupiter rumbled across the sky three times and three times the lightning flared.

The next day they set about exploring the countryside and, under Aeneas' direction, they constructed a strong military camp to defend themselves against possible attack. Aeneas also took the precaution of sending ambassadors to King Latinus, with gifts. Latinus received them well and asked the purpose of the Trojan visit to his land. The leader of the ambassadors explained how destiny had driven them there after the destruction of distant Troy. With the words of the oracle still fresh in his mind the King said, 'I have been expecting you, so tell your Aeneas to come himself. He can be sure of a welcome. Besides I want him to meet my daughter.'

He sent them back with a fine horse each, and for Aeneas a chariot drawn by two even finer animals. Joyfully they rode back with their message of peace. Several days later Aeneas visited the King and met Lavinia. The two men talked of many things and at last parted on very good terms. Latinus was delighted, convinced that he had found the perfect son-in-law.

However, Juno, from her place above the clouds, saw the success of Aeneas and his Trojan comrades. The very sight of them sitting comfortably on dry land made her blaze with anger. All her efforts to stop them had failed and she felt useless. Then a new idea came to her; she would summon Allecto, daughter of Pluto, from the depths of Tartarus. Allecto, the most terrible of the Furies, delighted in all the griefs and terrors of war. At Juno's bidding she began to destroy the newly-made peace between the Trojans and the Latins and to make both long for battle.

First she infected Amata, the Latin Queen, with her venom, poisoning her heart and mind. The poor Queen went quite mad, hid her daughter away in the forest, then went about the city stirring the women to furious hatred of the Trojans. Then Allecto flew straight to the city of Turnus, the young man who had hoped to marry Lavinia. While he slept the wicked Fury possessed his mind and spoke to him through a dream.

'How can you let this foreigner take what is rightly yours?' she asked. 'Take up arms and destroy the Trojans quickly.' Cunningly she twisted his thoughts and made him want war more than anything else. He awoke with a start, full of rage and began to prepare his army for battle. He felt only hatred and jealousy for the people he now considered dangerous invaders and he was determined to protect Italy from the Trojan threat.

Allecto, her dark wings hissing with snakes, then made her mischief among the countryfolk of Latium, stirring them to thoughts of war against the Trojans. Any small incident quickly led to a bitter quarrel, with Latins and Trojans gathering in force against each other, swords drawn, each side ready to kill.

In the city King Latinus found himself surrounded by people all mindlessly clamouring for war. They were encouraged by Turnus, newly arrived with his army, and eager for action. Latinus tried to reason with them but it was useless. In the end the frail old man gave up and shut himself away in his palace.

The custom in those times (as in the days of Imperial Rome) was to open the twin gates of war as soon as conflict began. Since Latinus refused to declare war on Aeneas and open the gates, Juno herself descended and jubilantly pushed them open. At this signal, all the tribes of Italy furiously prepared for war. Workshops up and down the land hummed with activity, producing weapons and armour for the men who massed in their thousands ready to march or ride into battle.

The trumpets sounded, the cry for war went up and chieftains led forth their ranks of soldiers. From the high mountain pastures and the fields of fertile river valleys they came to join the throng. More flocked in from the fishing villages of the coastlands, from the olive groves and the apple orchards. There were Oscans, Sabines and Saticulans, men from Feronia and Satura, and warriors of the Rutuli and the Sicani. Some carried javelins and short stabbing-spears, others had slings or bows with quivers bristling with arrows. Many had scimitars or heavy throwing-clubs, both deadly in battle. Rank upon rank of foot soldiers set out across the plains, making the earth shake as they marched. Troops of cavalry joined the infantry and numerous chariots, too, drawn by the finest horses.

Among the chieftains and famous warriors who gathered their armies behind Turnus was a girl called Camilla who came leading a column of bronze-armoured horsemen. She was the only daughter of a king named Metabus who had ruled in the city of Privernum in another part of Italy. Metabus was a tyrannical king and his people had eventually turned against him. To escape certain death he ran away into the mountains, taking his baby daughter Camilla with him. Soldiers pursued him for days and finally trapped him. In front was a wildly flowing river, swollen with rain and melting snow; behind, gaining every second, were the soldiers. Alone, he could have swum across the river but not with a baby. Then he realized what he had to do. Taking his spear he fastened the child securely to it, wrapping her round with layers of cork bark. He balanced the shaft ready to throw, then prayed to Diana the Huntress, 'I dedicate this child to you. Please, goddess, carry her safely across.' With that he sent the spear hurtling over the roaring water and saw it land safely before diving into the icy river and swimming across himself. Metabus lived for the rest of his life in those wild mountain forests, training his Camilla in the skills of hunting and war. True to his promise, he offered her to Diana and she grew up as the faithful servant and companion of the woodland goddess. It was, however, much against Diana's wishes that she now rode out to fight against the Trojans.

With all his supporters assembled around the Latin stronghold, Turnus was now ready for battle. He raised his flag of war above the city, boldly signalling the beginning of hostilities. Juno's wish was granted.

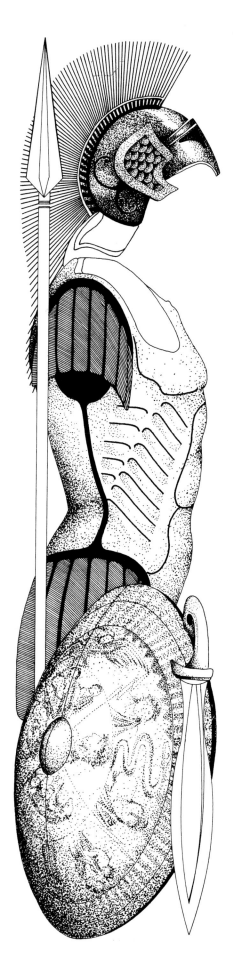

The site of Rome

While Turnus and his armies were massing around the Latin city, the Trojans made their own preparations for a war which now seemed inevitable. The days were spent in strengthening the camp fortifications, in sharpening weapons and laying in stores of food in case of a siege. At night, around the flickering fires, the men who had fought at Troy boasted of their adventures while the young boys, longing for their own first real battles, listened eagerly.

For Aeneas it was a time of great anxiety. As leader he was responsible for the lives of his people and he felt his responsibilities keenly, worrying about the new dangers which they all faced. One night he lay awake, unable to sleep and finally got up to walk in the night air. He spoke to each of the sentries who kept watch round the camp, then wandered down to the river bank. There he sat, staring at the dark water, then lay down full length and fell into a kind of uneasy half sleep. In his half dreaming state he saw a misty shape rising from the river.

'I am Tiberinus, god of this river,' said the grey form. 'This land has waited a long time for you, divine Prince and it is here that you are destined to make your home. Nearby your son Ascanius will build his city, a city with the shining name of Alba. But all this lies in the future. Now you have a difficult time to face and you need friends to help you. Row up my river tomorrow until you come to the township of Pallanteum where Evander the Arcadian rules. He is descended from your old enemies, the Greeks but he will be your best ally. Before you leave in the morning you will find a pure white sow feeding thirty piglets. Make sure you sacrifice these to Juno for she is so quick in her anger against you.'

Aeneas slept then and awoke only when the first rays of sunshine lit the eastern sky. Filled with new determination, he set about following the river god's instructions. He equipped two of his ships for the journey, then sacrificed the sow and her piglets which some of the Trojans had found near the river bank, not far from the place where the fleet was anchored. Then Aeneas and a group of specially chosen warriors boarded the ships and set off. Ascanius and the other Trojans watched until the ships had disappeared round the first bend, then returned to their own tasks.

At first the Trojans rowed vigorously upstream but soon they realized that the river itself was helping them on their journey; instead of flowing swiftly down to the sea, the waters were standing still to allow them to pass more easily.

It was evening when the Trojans arrived. The people of the town had gathered in a nearby grove of trees to celebrate the festival of their protector Hercules and the Trojans called greetings from the ships before approaching. They carried olive branches to show that they came in peace and Evander and his son Pallas stepped out of the crowd to meet them. Aeneas explained how the Latins had at first welcomed him but had then suddenly turned against him and were now preparing to drive him away. 'The Latins are no friends of ours,' said Evander. 'Come, join our feast now and tomorrow we will talk of war.'

The Trojans were given places of honour at the feast and as night settled over the sacred poplar grove, the ceremonies began again. Led by the King, the priests made fresh offerings at the altars, wearing leaves entwined in their hair and carrying flaming torches in their hands.

Singing and feasting lasted well into the night but at last the festival was over and at first light, they all walked back towards the city. Aeneas walked with Evander and Pallas, talking of the past and of how Evander, like Aeneas, had been driven from his homeland and led by the Fates to Italy. On the way they passed several impressive ruins, the remains of earlier settlements. 'In the old days,' explained Evander, 'only fauns and nymphs lived in these woods, with a race of primitive men who came from the trees. They were quite uncivilized in those days. They did not know how to sow crops or preserve food for the winter. They had no laws and just lived as they pleased, fighting each other for what they could get. Then Saturn came from heaven to live here and taught them how to live like human beings. Gradually they learned the skills of farming and lived in peace with one another in a golden age of plenty. Such prosperity could not last for ever, though, and gradually man's old nature returned: they began to long for more and more wealth, to fight and kill again for power

and gold. One tyrant king replaced another as evil as the one before and so it continued until I myself was driven here.'

Although Aeneas did not realize it, he was wandering across the place which in later times was to be the site of great Rome itself. Much of it was overgrown with trees and thick undergrowth but among the tangle of bushes were places which were to become famous landmarks in the city. There was the grove where Romulus was to take refuge, and the cave nearby called the Lupercal or Wolf's Cave. There, too, was the rocky cliff that came to be called the Tarpeian rock and, most important of all, the spot where the temple of Jupiter Capitolinus was to stand. From Evander's own house Aeneas looked down to the plain below, dotted with cattle grazing in the early sun; in years to come the Roman Forum was to be built there, the great market place and meeting point of Rome. Finally, Evander showed Aeneas to his room and, exhausted by the night's festivities, he fell deeply asleep.

Far away in the home of the gods, Venus was as usual worrying about her son, especially now that so many dangers were threatening his safety. Her husband was Vulcan, the master of fire, and as they lay together in their golden bedroom, she asked him to use his great skill in metalwork to forge weapons for Aeneas. Venus had her own skill in the arts of womanly persuasion and before long Vulcan had reluctantly agreed to her request. Early the next morning he rose refreshed from sleep and made his way to his forge, deep in a cave beneath the island called Vulcania, not far from Mount Etna. There three giant one-eyed Cyclopes worked, making all the things the gods required: one was hammering out a thunderbolt for Jupiter, another finishing a chariot for Mars, the third fashioning armour for Minerva. 'Lay all this work aside,' commanded Vulcan, 'and put your strength and skill to a new task. We have weapons to make for a hero!'

Soon molten metal ran in rivers and the cavern resounded to the rhythm of hammer blows and the roar of the furnaces. The Cyclopes worked as a team, shaping the helmet, shield and breastplate, forging the sword and spear and burnishing the leg armour until it gleamed.

Unaware of all this activity, Evander and Aeneas woke to find the sun already high in the sky. With no time to lose, they sat down with Evander's son Pallas and Aeneas' companion Achates, to discuss the next move. Evander spoke first:

'Great captain of the Trojans, you have come to us seeking an ally. You may certainly have our support, but this is a small, poor kingdom and we cannot offer you a large fighting force. However, we have powerful neighbours, the Etruscans, and I know they have a good reason for joining you. Not long ago they were ruled by a terrible tyrant called Mezentius. When they rebelled against him he escaped and he now lives under the protection of your enemy Turnus. The strange hand of Fate has brought you here at the very time when they are preparing themselves for war to recapture him and punish him for his crimes. They are ready for action but await a man who is strong enough to lead them.'

'Are there no Etruscans who can take on the task?' asked Aeneas.

'There are many who would be willing and able but a warning from the gods makes them wait for a commander who is not of their race. They asked me if I would do it, but you can see I am too old.' Evander paused to look intently at Aeneas. 'Now you are just the man. They will accept you without question, so go to them at once and take my son with you to help you.'

Aeneas was considering this new suggestion when his mother gave him a clear sign of approval. The blue morning sky was suddenly torn by great flashes of lightning and thunder boomed out like the sound of war trumpets. In a bank of high-piled clouds, the watchers saw the glint of weapons, heard the clash of swords and spears in the air. Everyone was afraid but Aeneas understood the meaning of the sign and reassured them that it was favourable to him. Thanking his mother for her support, he relit the altar fire and made the necessary offerings before sending his ships back down the river to the Trojan camp to tell them of his plans.

Aeneas kept a group of his bravest soldiers to go with him to the Etruscans and Evander provided a squadron of horsemen led by his son Pallas. Soon they were ready to set out. Aeneas mounted a horse specially chosen for him by the King and the party rode out across the dusty plain to the place where the Etruscans were camped. The people who were left behind watched them go with a strange sense of sadness. Evander was worried for the safety of his son while the mothers and wives of the other men stood forlornly on the battlements watching their menfolk disappear into the distance. Who could tell how or when they would return?

Negotiations with the Etruscans went well. They had heard of Aeneas' adventures and welcomed him as the champion they had been expecting. They eagerly agreed to join his cause against Turnus and were soon sending messengers to the towns and cities around to muster an impressive army.

As the Etruscan commanders sat down with the Trojans to discuss battle plans, Aeneas wandered off by himself to a quiet wood nearby. He needed to think carefully about the dangers he knew he must soon face. As he walked deeper into the wood, he saw a shining figure descending among the leaves ahead of him. It was Venus, carrying the magnificent armour and weapons that Vulcan had now completed. She laid them down under a tree and vanished as quickly as she had come.

Aeneas approached the tree reverently and picked up each shining piece of armour in turn, wondering at the fineness of their workmanship: the helmet with its fiery red plumes, the glowing breastplate made of bronze, the death-dealing sword and spear, the leg armour which fitted his legs exactly and was finished in smooth gold alloy. To Aeneas the most amazing object of all was the shield, for on this the fire god Vulcan had skilfully engraved pictures showing the whole future story of Rome. The people who were to be his descendants and whose faces he had seen so recently in the Underworld, were all vividly portrayed in lifelike detail and Aeneas looked at them in wonder, filled with a sense of destiny. At last he lifted the shield on his arm to feel its weight and balance, quietly pitying those who were fated to oppose him. Then, still brooding on the future, he made his way back to the Etruscan camp.

The siege

While Aeneas was away seeking support from the Etruscans, Turnus saw his opportunity and marched towards the Trojan camp to attack it while its greatest warrior was out of the way. The watchful Trojans saw the Italian army while it was still just a black smudge on the distant horizon. At once the alarm was raised. Men appeared from all directions to line the ramparts, their weapons at the ready. Then the gates were closed tightly and barred against attack. The Trojans' first impulse was to march out and meet the enemy in the open, but Aeneas had left strict orders that if they were attacked while he was away they should only defend the camp and stay shut within its wooden palisade.

Turnus, impatient to begin the battle, rode some distance ahead of the main force, flanked by twenty powerful bodyguards. Wearing a golden helmet plumed with red and riding a fine war horse, he threw a javelin into the air to show that the fighting should start. To the sound of cheers and chilling war-cries, he rode wildly round and round the camp, searching for a way in. He had expected the Trojans to be outside the palisade, ready for open battle, not huddled like cowards inside it and he was furious to find every entrance barred against him. He began to call out insults to the Trojans, daring them to come out and fight like men but they just stared down coldly at him from the ramparts and refused to be moved.

Meanwhile the rest of his army had arrived and was drawn up in readiness, rank upon rank of disciplined fighting men. There was little they could do unless the Trojans could be lured out of their stronghold and eventually Turnus thought he saw how this could be done. Near the camp, secured to the river bank behind a low defensive earthwork, was the Trojan fleet. Quickly, Turnus shouted his orders.

'Make blazing torches. We'll burn their precious ships, then they'll be certain to fight. They shall not escape us now.'

As the Trojans watched helplessly, the Italian soldiers gathered up pinewood firebrands and dashed towards the ships with Turnus in the lead. What happened next surprised the Trojans as much as it did the Italians.

The wood which Aeneas had used to build his fleet had come from the sacred grove of the mother goddess, Cybele. She had given it freely to him but was determined now that it should not be destroyed. The sturdy planks and beams of pine, maple and hard oak had completed their task of carrying Aeneas and his people to safety and Jupiter now gave Cybele permission to turn the ships into goddesses of the sea. As Turnus approached the ships, a burning torch in each hand, a bright light blazed in the sky and from the east came a great, fast-moving cloud, alive with the music of Cybele. Turnus and his men stood still, frozen in the very act of throwing their flames, as an awesome voice echoed from the cloud: 'Do not arm yourselves, Trojans, to defend my ships. They are safe from Turnus and from all who wish them harm.' Then she spoke to the ships themselves. 'Now, goddesses of the sea, go, for your mother commands you to swim free.'

At once the ships began to toss and twist at their moorings until each one broke free and plunged dolphin-like beneath the water. When the flurry of waves had died down, the ships had vanished and in their place were a shoal of water nymphs, darting playfully near the shore, dancing in the water before swimming away towards the open sea.

The Italian soldiers were terrified but Turnus was unruffled by the strange transformation. Confidently he called out to his men, 'These portents should make the Trojan cowards tremble, not us. Don't you understand? Jupiter himself has removed their means of escape; they are trapped, with only a wooden stockade and a puny ditch to hide behind. This is a second Troy! But we don't need tricks and wooden horses to destroy it. We are not Greeks, who need ten years to vanquish a city. No, one day will be enough for us! Tomorrow will see the end of this Trojan rabble.'

By this time night was falling and Turnus gave orders for his troops to surround the Trojan camp so that no-one could escape. A ring of watch-fires was lit and men were detailed to stay on guard throughout the night. In this temporary camp the soldiers rested. They ate, drank wine and, satisfied that all was secure, stretched out on the grass to sleep.

Inside the Trojan camp, however, no-one had time to sleep; there was too much to do to prepare for the determined attack which they knew would come the next day. The gates and wooden walls were checked and rechecked, weapons were polished and sharpened and battle theories endlessly discussed. Without Aeneas to lead and encourage them they felt anxious and afraid, uncertain whether to obey his instructions or to take the initiative and fight on the open ground. The commanders would have liked to send word somehow to Aeneas, warning him of what had happened but there was no way through the enemy lines. The situation seemed hopeless.

Among those standing guard that night were two young Trojans, Nisus and Euryalus, inseparable friends who were both eager to prove themselves. Like everyone else they talked about what to do and they decided to ask the commanders if they could go to find Aeneas. Impressed by their courage, the leaders accepted the offer gratefully. Here at last was something positive for them to do.

Nisus and Euryalus were lowered silently over the wooden palisade, then crept across the defensive ditches, carefully making their way through the darkness. The watch-fires had burned to a low glimmer and the whole enemy army by then lay in a drunken sleep, quite unprotected. The two Trojans did not hesitate but moved from group to group, stabbing and slashing at the sleeping soldiers as they went to make sure that no-one raised the alarm and followed them.

At last, as the moon rose over the trees, they knew it was time to be on their way. They collected as many weapons as they could carry and made for the shelter of the woods. It was too late! Their quick movements and the glint of metal from their helmets in the moonlight betrayed them to a passing company of Italian cavalry, returning from a foraging expedition. 'Halt!' called the horsemen and, when the two did not stop, 'Halt or you are dead.'

Nisus and Euryalus ran desperately into the dark tangle of undergrowth with the horsemen in hot pursuit. Nisus managed to escape further into the woods but Euryalus was caught in the thorns and was soon surrounded by angry

Italians. Rather than leave his friend to face the enemy alone Nisus returned cautiously and, peering through the leaves, saw Euryalus struggling to free himself. Muttering a hasty prayer to Diana the huntress, he threw two spears in quick succession at the horsemen. Each found its mark and two Italians fell dead. Their leader grabbed Euryalus roughly and raised his sword to kill him as Nisus shouted from his hiding place and ran forward to try to save him. 'Don't blame him,' he cried desperately. 'I am the leader here. I am responsible. Let me die.' But the horsemen were merciless and in an instant the two brave friends lay dead under a rain of blows.

Early the next day Turnus rallied his troops ready for a new attack. The discovery of so many soldiers lying dead around the watch-fires made the survivors doubly eager for battle and doubly determined to break into the guarded camp. From their positions on the ramparts the Trojans heard the urgent blare of the war trumpets and prepared to repel the first rush of soldiers beneath the walls.

The enemy moved forward like a giant tortoise, sheltering under a roof of shields, carrying ladders with which they intended to scale the walls. From a distance, archers shot volleys of arrows to give the attackers covering fire and to try to prevent the Trojan defenders

from rolling huge stones down from the wall onto the struggling mass of soldiers below. In one place they threw blazing torches into the camp, setting fire to one side of a tall wooden tower crowded with soldiers. The flames brought it crashing down in a splintering mass, sending showers of sparks and burning splinters into the camp.

Many brave men on both sides died that day as the battle raged furiously on. Ascanius, Aeneas' son, was always in the most dangerous positions, where the fighting was fiercest. Until that day he had only used his weapons against wild animals and in practice with other young men; now he was pitting his strength and skill against experienced soldiers. One man in particular caught his attention for he was boldly parading up and down outside the gates, shouting insults and boasting of the Trojans he had killed. Angrily, Ascanius loosed a deadly arrow which flew straight to the man's head. As the boaster fell to the ground, the Trojans roared their approval, encouraged by the boy's example.

All this time the gods were closely watching the progress of the battle. Juno was urging on Turnus and his soldiers while Venus whispered advice and encouragement to the besieged Trojans. Now, seeing Ascanius exposing himself to danger, she called on Apollo to assist her. Swifter than light he descended, disguised, to the Trojan camp and came quickly up to where Ascanius was standing.

'Take care, Ascanius,' he warned. 'Your courage is great and there is no doubt that men like you are badly needed in the fight. But you also have a greater role to play. The future of your people depends on you; so do not endanger yourself unnecessarily. Be brave but not foolhardy and all will be well.'

Reluctantly the boy agreed and Apollo then disappeared as swiftly as he had come.

The battle seemed to rage like a fierce storm, reaching a new and wilder pitch as the day wore on. Then, against all orders, two fiery young Trojan brothers, Pandarus and Bitias, in a sudden fit of bravado, opened the gate they were guarding and stood ready at the entrance, challenging anyone who dared to enter. The enemy, who had been waiting for just such a chance, rushed for the gap but were repelled again and again by the brothers who stood tall and firm as trees on either side. Now Turnus saw his chance of victory. Riding furiously across the battlefield, he charged straight in at the open gateway, striking down Trojans to right and left. Bitias stood in his path but a siege ball, thrown by one of the groups of attacking Italians, struck him like a meteor and knocked him senseless to the ground.

Encouraged by Turnus and strengthened by the support of Mars and Juno, the Italians now pressed on with even greater force, sensing victory was within their grasp. Some of the Trojans ventured out to beat off the attackers so that when at last Pandarus managed to push the gate closed, he shut out many of his own soldiers. Inside, however, he trapped Turnus who, relishing a new challenge, raged like an angry tiger, forcing his way deeper and deeper into the camp, scattering Trojans in every direction.

At last the Trojan leaders managed to rally their forces, shouting words of encouragement to one another above the noise of clanging swords and shields. Turnus was surrounded by a close rank of troops and although he repeatedly broke free, he was eventually forced back by sheer weight of numbers. The gates were reopened to expel him and he was pushed towards the river bank, alone among an angry mass of Trojans. His own men shrank before their fury and Turnus was driven slowly backwards. He fought bravely as the blows rained down on his shield, helmet and armour but gradually his strength began to fail. Looking desperately over his shoulder he saw that there was only one way he could escape now and he leaped, still fully armed, into the river Tiber.

It was not the end of the battle for Turnus, however, for he had powerful gods on his side. The water of the Tiber supported him gently, despite the weight of his armour. Washing him clean of sweat and blood, it carried him gently downstream, reviving him with its eddying currents. Once safely away from the battle it floated him to the shore where he climbed the bank, refreshed and ready to fight again.

The great battle

The war that raged so fiercely around the Trojan encampment on the banks of the Tiber caused consternation in heaven. Jupiter called the gods and goddesses around his throne to discuss the situation, angry because his plans for peace in Italy had been disregarded. Venus was quick to remind him that it was Juno who had tried to destroy the Trojans and the Queen of Heaven for her part passionately defended her actions.

'What crime have I committed?' she asked proudly. 'These peaceful Italians are threatened by the Trojan invaders and naturally fear for their land. All I did was lend my support to a just cause.'

The gods were deeply divided by the argument. Some took one side, some the other and there was a loud hum of conversation in the great hall. Then silence fell as the Lord of Creation spoke.

'Hear what I have decided. Since both these forces seem intent on war, let the Fates decide what will happen. I will not take sides and neither must any of you. Leave them both alone and may the most deserving win the victory.'

With a look that made further discussion out of the question, Jupiter left the assembly.

Back on earth, Aeneas, quite unaware of the desperate plight of his countrymen, was sailing towards them at the head of the Etruscan fleet, bringing a great army to confront the Latins and the Rutulians in open battle. Tarchon, the Etruscan King, had welcomed Aeneas as the long-awaited leader and an alliance had quickly been made. All the Etruscan cities had sent strong contingents and soldiers crowded onto the galleys of the war fleet, eager to take on the enemy.

It was during the voyage south along the coast that a strange event took place. Aeneas, worrying as usual and unable to sleep, was alone at the helm of his ship as it sailed gently under a moonlit sky. Suddenly the water all round was alive with nymphs, splashing and playing in the waves. They were the same nymphs that Cybele had created from the Trojan ships and they recognized Aeneas, dancing around his vessel with delight. One of them, Cymodoce, spoke to Aeneas, explaining who they were and telling him how Turnus had besieged the Trojan camp in his absence. Then, still dancing in the waves, they swam with the fleet, helping the ships on their way.

By the time dawn broke they were within sight of the Trojan camp and could see the bustle of the soldiers and hear the sounds of an army preparing for another day's battle. Aeneas raised his gold-rimmed shield and flashed a signal to his countrymen. At once a brave cry echoed from within the camp as the Trojans realized that help was on the way. The Rutulians also heard the shout and looking round to see what had caused it, saw the ships heading swiftly towards them.

Turnus, as confident and courageous as ever, ordered his army to leave the besieged camp and march to attack the Etruscans as they came ashore. Once more the trumpets blared as the ships prepared to land. As they ran into shallow water, the men jumped out, leaping through the waves to gain a firm footing on the sand. Aeneas was the first to lead a charge into the waiting army and he fought like a man inspired. No-one, however strong or however skilled in the arts of battle, could stand against him and he fought like ten warriors as he forced a way through the Rutulian lines.

Further along the beach, Pallas, Evander's son, led his cavalry into the thick of the fighting. This was his first taste of battle and he, too, fought magnificently, inspiring his followers to perform great deeds themselves. Turnus, fighting on another part of the shore, kept a watchful general's eye on the progress of the battle and he soon noticed the damage that Pallas and his cavalry were inflicting on his troops. He sped across the battlefield in his chariot and ordered his men to fall back.

'Pallas, son of Evander,' he roared, 'let us settle our quarrel like heroes, you and I. Call off your men and stand to fight in single combat. I, Turnus, challenge you.'

The two men stood to face each other, spears poised. Pallas was the first to throw but his spear did nothing more than graze Turnus' shoulder. Then Turnus threw his weapon. His aim was so true and his thrust so powerful that the spear passed straight through Pallas' shield and struck him full in the chest; he fell dead instantly. Soldiers of both sides gathered round as Turnus triumphantly strode over to the body and roughly removed a wide, studded sword-belt as a trophy. Then as the men turned to continue the

fight, a group of Pallas' soldiers lifted his body carefully onto a shield and carried it sadly away.

News of the death of Pallas spread swiftly through the Trojan and Etruscan ranks and when Aeneas heard what had happened he was filled with grief and anger. He remembered the warm welcome Pallas' father Evander had given him, the friendship and support that had guided him to his Etruscan allies and given him Evander's only son to fight a stranger's cause. How the old man would suffer now! There was no time for grief, however, in the middle of war and, gripping his sword and shield more firmly, Aeneas strode across the battlefield like a whirlwind, scattering the enemy in all directions. His one aim was to find Turnus and kill him.

The gods had been forbidden to interfere in the struggle below but they continued to observe what was happening with as much interest as ever. As Aeneas raged towards Turnus, Juno could stay silent no longer.

'Great lord and husband,' she pleaded, 'grant me one simple request. Let me take Turnus away from this madman; let me save him from the wrath of Aeneas.'

Jupiter thought for a moment. 'Your Turnus is destined to die, you must realize that. All I can grant you is a reprieve, nothing more. His fate is fixed.'

'There is just a chance that you will change your mind and grant my Rutulian a long life,' replied Juno. 'I cannot give up that hope.'

Hurrying to the battlefield, she arranged for Aeneas to be delayed in his hunt for Turnus. Then, near the spot from which Turnus was directing the battle, she created out of cloud a shadowy figure which was the exact likeness of Aeneas, complete with all his special armour.

The apparition proudly challenged Turnus to fight and Turnus was completely deceived by it. He sprang forward at once but the shadow Aeneas turned away from him and ran towards the ships drawn up on the beach. Turnus followed close behind. The shadow climbed a ladder onto one of the ships and disappeared inside it.

'Aeneas,' cried Turnus, clambering aboard after it, 'come out and fight me like a man. Where are

you skulking? Come out and fight, I say.'

As soon as Turnus was on the ship, however, Juno swept it out to sea on a freak wave. The shadow Aeneas evaporated into the air and Turnus found himself drifting helplessly away from the shore. The sounds of shouting and the clang of weapons and shields grew fainter as the ship gathered speed and there was nothing that Turnus could do to stop it. He knew that everyone would despise him for deserting the battlefield and, in despair, he tried three times to kill himself. Each time Juno prevented his death and at last, exhausted, he fell asleep on the deck.

The Etruscan army had joined forces with Aeneas not simply to assist him in his cause but also to confront the tyrant King Mezentius who had been living under the protection of Turnus. Once firmly established on the beach, they began to search for him among the enemy officers. At last they saw him and closed in to make an attack in force. Mezentius, however, was a great fighter and he withstood all their blows without flinching, killing many of the Etruscans in return.

Aeneas, frustrated because he could not find Turnus, saw a group of struggling Etruscans surrounding an imposing warrior and ran towards them, weapons at the ready. Mezentius saw him coming and sent his spear hissing through the air towards him but Aeneas' shield was already raised in defence and the spear glanced off it to one side. Then Aeneas cast his spear. The weapon, forged by the Cyclopes in the furnace of the gods, flew directly to its mark, penetrating Mezentius' bronze shield and striking him in the groin. He staggered back and fell, bleeding. Aeneas pulled out his sword and leaped forward to take his life.

Before Aeneas could strike, however, a young boy had flung himself between Aeneas and the wounded man and had bravely taken the first sword blow on his up-raised shield. It was Mezentius' son, Lausus, who had watched the encounter with horror and moved instinctively to protect his father.
'Go, father,' he cried. 'I will hold this Trojan upstart. Escape while there is time.'

As Mezentius crawled painfully away, Aeneas

73

drew back, unwilling to injure the boy.
'Stand and fight, Trojan,' cried Lausus. 'Must I show you how warriors behave?'

Aeneas could not ignore Lausus' challenge but still he tried to discourage him.
'You are courting certain death,' he told him. 'You have behaved like a hero but leave now, go to comfort your father. You are more help to him alive than dead.'

Still the boy persisted in his defiance and finally Aeneas could not hold back any longer. Raising his deadly sword he thrust it clean through Lausus' shield and into his heart, killing him outright. Then, full of pity for the boy's courage, he lifted him gently onto a shield and commanded the Etruscans to carry him to Mezentius.

The tyrant King was resting by the river, leaning on a tree trunk, gasping with pain and calling out for his son. When they brought him Lausus' body, grief and anger gave him new strength. Wounded as he was, he struggled to buckle on his armour and sword and called for his horse. He was determined to avenge his son's death or die in the attempt. Grasping a javelin in each hand, he galloped back into the battle and loudly called his challenge to Aeneas.

Mezentius found Aeneas standing ready for the fight and rode in a wide circle around him, throwing the two javelins in rapid succession. Aeneas skilfully caught them both on his shield and, unharmed, took careful aim with his own spear at Mezentius' horse. As the spear pierced its forehead, the animal reared into the air then fell heavily to the ground, trapping Mezentius under its body. Aeneas ran forward, his sword raised for the final blow. This time the tyrant would not escape.
'You will kill me, I know,' gasped Mezentius, 'and I do not fear to die. Just allow me one thing. Do not leave my body to the Etruscans for they hate me so much they will treat me like a dog. You are the only one who can grant me the favour of a proper burial.'
'It shall be as you ask,' said Aeneas then, with a single powerful thrust of his sword, he sent the tyrant to the world of the dead.

This decisive event ended the battle. Turnus had vanished, Mezentius was dead and the Rutulians were left without a leader; the Trojans and Etruscans had won the day. Quietly the men of both sides withdrew to their camps to dress their wounds and recover from the horrors of the day. Both victors and vanquished were exhausted by the long struggle and whether flushed with success or sunk in despair, all slept early around the campfires.

The next morning Aeneas rose early and set to work on a great trophy to honour Mars the god of war. The massive armour of Mezentius was displayed in a prominent place and when the army had gathered round, Aeneas spoke to them all, praising them for their valour and encouraging them to fight on to final and lasting victory. 'We have won a great battle, but we are not yet secure in Italy,' he told them. 'Our next task is to march to the city of Latium and face the enemy on their own ground. Otherwise they will certainly return to harass us again. But first we must respect the unburied bodies of our brave comrades. Let full funeral rites be performed for them so that their spirits may rest in peace. Remember, too, that it is not only Trojans who have died. Remember Pallas, the brave son of Evander, who died fighting for our cause. Let his body be returned with all honour to his home.'

Weeping at the thought of this sad homecoming and of Evander's despair at losing his only son, the sole heir to his kingdom, Aeneas chose a thousand men to accompany Pallas on his last journey. The body was wrapped in purple cloth and laid on a bier of wickerwork. With them the soldiers carried all the spoils of war, the horses, chariots and weapons which they had captured from the Rutulians, a melancholy tribute to the young man's courage.

Aeneas watched the long procession disappear along the road, then saluted Pallas for the last time. He returned to the Trojan camp to find envoys arrived from the enemy to arrange for the burial of their soldiers killed in the battle. A twelve-day truce was agreed to give time for all the funeral rites to be performed.

Men from both sides then began the same sad tasks. In the woods nearby they began felling trees for the funeral pyres. The timber was

encouraged them all to attack Aeneas, was still mysteriously missing and it seemed that everyone had a different suggestion for bringing the war to an end. Some wanted to continue fighting and drive the Trojans back to the sea; others wanted to exile Turnus and welcome Aeneas—so ending the war immediately. Yet others believed that Aeneas and Turnus (when he reappeared) should decide the issue in single combat. Another idea was to offer the Trojans a strip of coastland on which they could settle—or even a new fleet in which to sail away in search of another land. The arguments raged endlessly until Turnus himself returned, as eager for battle as ever, and easily swayed the majority in his favour. He was confident that this time he would lead his army to an overwhelming victory.

When the funeral rites had been completed and the time of truce was at an end, Aeneas set out with his army towards Latium. He sent his cavalry divisions across the open plain but led the bulk of his army, the foot soldiers, by a different route through rough hill-country. News of his approach spread quickly through the city making everyone anxious and excited. The conference in the palace ended with no real battle plan agreed and the people armed themselves, panicking as they prepared to defend the city. It was Turnus who took charge of the situation. He supervised the manning of the walls and towers of the city, enlisting the help of every able-bodied male, both young and old. Then he ordered his troops, infantry and cavalry, to stand ready in their companies on the plain by the city, poised and ready for action at any moment.

When all the preparations were at last completed, Turnus, clad in armour of shining bronze and gold, assembled his personal bodyguards. He was about to set out for the plain when Camilla appeared, leading her cavalry squadron. She jumped down from her horse and stood before him.
'Turnus, these brave men request your permission to ride ahead with me and engage the enemy cavalry. That will leave you free to command the infantry in the rear and stay close to defend the city.'

Turnus was impressed by Camilla's courage

carted down to the shore in wagonloads and piled up in great heaps. The bodies of the dead soldiers were laid on the pyres and fires were kindled at their bases. As the smoke rose, trumpets sounded and cries of mourning filled the air. Onto the flames they threw all the equipment of war which littered the field of battle while nearby, animals were sacrificed to appease the god of death. For a whole day and night the mourners stood watching as the fires burned themselves slowly out. When only smouldering heaps remained, the bones and ashes were collected and buried together in a mass grave beneath a huge barrow of earth. For twelve days there was peace.

Meanwhile, matters were far from happy in Latium. The people there mourned the loss of so many of those dear to them while in the palace the King and his advisers argued constantly over what should be done. Turnus, who had and knowledge of war. 'Brave Camilla,' he said, 'we shall share today's great task. My plan is to ambush the army of Aeneas in the hills. He is a stranger to these parts and knows nothing of the countryside. I know an ideal place to trap him. While I am tackling him there, you shall lead all the cavalry divisions of our invincible army and engage the enemy's charging horsemen. May the gods go with you!'

Turnus set off with his men for the hills, leaving Camilla in charge of the cavalry. The whole host quivered with excitement, eager for battle and as the enemy cavalry appeared on the horizon, she commanded her horsemen to advance at speed on a broad front. They raced forward, pounding the plain with the incessant drumming of their horses' feet, filling the air with the wild shouts of battle. As the two sides drew nearer each other, spears were levelled and thrust forward for the deadly charge. Many fell in the confusion that followed when the lines of horsemen clashed for the first time. Then quite suddenly the Trojan line broke and at once Camilla gave the order to her men to turn around. Holding their shields against their backs to protect themselves, the horsemen rode furiously back towards the city with the Trojans in hot pursuit. Then, still in tight formation, they turned round again. The Trojans were taken completely by surprise and, unable to halt their headlong charge, they rode straight onto the enemy spears.

So the battle continued, back and forth across the plain, with now one side gaining an advantage, now the other. Among those who fought most furiously was Camilla herself, armed not just with Diana's golden bow but also with a spear and a strong battle-axe. Many men fell beneath her blows as she galloped across the battlefield. Everyone who challenged her met the same fate, so accurate were her spear-casts and so deadly the arrows that flew from her bow.

However, danger lurked constantly at Camilla's back, for an Etruscan called Arruns was watching her closely, waiting for his chance to catch her unawares. At last that chance came and he let fly his spear from a safe distance. The soldiers who were with Camilla looked up suddenly as they heard the hiss of the thrown spear and ducked safely out of its way but Camilla herself was oblivious to the danger. A moment later the sharpened point struck her just below the breast. Her men caught her as she fell forward from the saddle but the wound was fatal. Still her only thought was for the safety of the Italians and with her dying breath she ordered her closest companion to take a warning message to Turnus.

From high above, Diana saw her beloved Camilla die in the midst of the battle and she at once sent her nymph Opis to avenge the girl's death. The cowardly Arruns, his ambition fulfilled, had fled in fear to a quiet part of the battlefield but Opis found him and loosed an arrow which killed him instantly. He died unnoticed and alone.

Without the fearless Camilla to lead them, the Latins suddenly lost heart. They turned in confusion and began to retreat in complete disorder, making for the shelter of the city with the Trojan forces close behind them. The people left inside to defend the city had closed the gates tightly and the fleeing troops were trapped around the walls, unable to gain entry and equally unable to avoid the pursuing Trojans. The main force of the Latin cavalry was wiped out without pity.

While the cavalry were fighting on the plain, Turnus was lying in wait to ambush the rest of Aeneas' army who were advancing over the hills. Camilla's messenger found him well hidden at a point where Aeneas' men would have to pass through a narrow, steep-sided valley and hurriedly told him what had happened. The news of the defeat of his cavalry and of Camilla's death made Turnus angry and distressed. His first thought now was that he must save the city and he abandoned his ambush plans at once and marched his troops back towards Latium. It was only as he led his men onto the plain that he discovered the Trojan army was already close behind.

By this time the sun was sinking rapidly in the western sky so the two armies spread themselves on the plain before the city walls and rested, preparing themselves for a decisive battle on the following day.

The end of the war

After his hasty retreat to Latium, Turnus left his army camped for the night outside the city walls. He himself entered the city and was dismayed to find the people in very low spirits. They had watched the massacre of the Latin cavalry from the battlements and had lost many defenders to well-aimed enemy arrows. Their will to fight was almost gone and Turnus saw how they looked at him, their eyes full of loathing. In the palace he found King Latinus with the Queen and their daughter Lavinia beside him. Latinus appealed to Turnus, begging him to give up his claim to Lavinia and so end the war.

Turnus was furious. Words of reason only made him more determined to defeat Aeneas and he sent a message to the Trojan leader, challenging him to fight at dawn in single combat so that the issue could be decided once and for all.

Scarcely had the sun begun to touch the distant mountain peaks than the two armies took up positions to watch the contest. In the narrow gap between the opposing forces altars of turf had been set up by priests from both sides and fires lit in readiness for the rituals that would have to be performed. Then the two Kings, Latinus and Turnus appeared, riding in fine chariots. Turnus, wearing his shining armour of gold and bronze, drove a chariot drawn by two pure white war-horses and looked a truly formidable champion. Aeneas, with Ascanius beside him, stepped forward from the ranks of his men to meet them. Together they all offered sacrificial animals before the altars and prayed to the gods for their blessing. Then Aeneas and Latinus made a solemn treaty of peace.

'If Turnus wins this combat,' announced Aeneas, 'then my people will leave this land and make no further claims on it of any sort. If I win our two nations will join as equal partners, with Latinus as the supreme ruler. I shall take Lavinia as my bride and she will give her name to a new city that we Trojans will build. I swear this by all that is sacred.'

Latinus, too, swore to keep his side of the bargain. All was not well, however, among the ranks of the Latins who stood by to witness the ceremony. Juno had again interfered, this time by sending the sister of Turnus, the nymph Juturna, to do her bidding. Juturna's one aim was to protect her brother, so she moved among the Latin soldiers in disguise, spreading discontent and uncertainty, hinting that if Aeneas won, he would break the treaty and take over their lands completely. One of the soldiers became so maddened with desire to shed enemy blood that he took up his spear and threw it into the Trojan ranks.

The truce was broken and immediately each side surged forward, their lust for battle renewed. As Aeneas stood helpless among the crowd of furious fighting men, a stray arrow shot by one of Turnus' soldiers struck him in the leg. He fell with a cry of agony and was hurriedly carried from the field.

Turnus leaped into his chariot at once and drove forward into the very thick of the battle. Those who were not trampled to death by the flying hooves of his horses were mown down by his quick-flashing sword as he swept onwards, scenting victory.

Meanwhile, Trojan doctors were attending to Aeneas as he lay seriously wounded on the ground. Fortunately, they received divine assistance: Venus, ever watchful, came invisibly to the camp with a miraculous herbal cure which quickly healed Aeneas' wound. With his strength fully restored, he rode out onto the battlefield once more and his whole army rallied at the sight of him. But the Italians trembled with fear.

Aeneas' one desire was to confront Turnus and finish the fight once and for all but Juturna, still following Juno's orders, was determined that Turnus should escape his fate. She disguised herself as his charioteer and quickly took up the horses' reins, driving the chariot off at full speed, racing back and forth across the plain, always avoiding Aeneas. Time and again Aeneas approached the chariot, hoping to lure Turnus into combat, but each time it whirled away in a cloud of dust.

Aeneas was angry and insulted. Not only had the Italians broken the peace treaty, now their champion would not stand his ground and fight. He decided on a change of tactics and ordered his troops to make a concerted attack on the city itself. Immediately they moved in with ladders, blazing torches and battering rams, determined to raze the city to the ground. The gates were

soon forced open and the terrified citizens ran from house to house in panic as the Trojans entered, killing and looting as they penetrated to the heart of Latium.

From far out on the plain, Turnus looked back towards Latium. He saw the smoke rising from the burning buildings and heard the tumult. Realizing what had happened, he knew that he alone could save his people; he resolved to fight Aeneas and to accept his fate with courage. Still Juturna tried to prevent him but this time he was resolute. Seizing the reins himself, he drove to the city walls, then leaped down and ran into the city, charging through the tangle of soldiers around the gates, scattering men and weapons in all directions.

'It is I, Turnus,' he cried. 'Let the fighting cease. Aeneas, I challenge you once more to single combat. Come out and fight!'

The two great warriors circled round each other, cast their spears, then rushed forward like a pair of ferocious bulls. Their shields crashed and Turnus, seeing his chance to wound Aeneas, raised his sword ready to strike. As he brought it down heavily the blade snapped off and fell harmlessly to the ground. Turnus, desperate now, ran to his soldiers, demanding a new sword but Aeneas was too quick for him. With his own sword upraised, he shouted:

'This sword brings instant death to anyone who arms Turnus.'

The soldiers drew back, afraid, and Aeneas strode forward to retrieve his spear, then walked slowly and menacingly towards his enemy.

Jupiter and Juno were watching the climax of the Trojans' long battle, discussing the outcome of the conflict. Juno had at last realized how hopeless it was to pit her strength against the dictates of Fate. She promised not to cause any more trouble and then asked one favour.

'My lord,' she said, 'when peace is made and the two nations are joined in marriage, let the Latins retain their name, their language and their customs. Troy has fallen, so let her name remain buried forever.'

Jupiter readily agreed and at last Juno was content to let Fate take its course.

Outside the walls of Latium, Aeneas moved closer and closer to Turnus who stood, unarmed

Aeneas paused, unsure of his next action. As he hesitated, he noticed that Turnus was wearing as a trophy the belt that he had torn from the body of Pallas and his heart hardened.

'Remember Pallas,' Aeneas cried, 'for it is he who takes his revenge on you now.'

Without another word he raised his mighty sword and with a single blow killed the man who had opposed him so bitterly. As his body grew limp and cold, the spirit of Turnus left the world of the living and flew to the land of eternal shadow.

It is here that Virgil's long poem telling the adventures of Aeneas comes to an end but the story of what happened next, and how Aeneas became established in Italy, is taken up by Livy, the Roman historian. According to his account, the death of Turnus brought the war dramatically to an end. Aeneas and Latinus confirmed their treaty of peace and Aeneas duly married the beautiful Lavinia, so joining his Trojans to the Latins and making them a single people. From that time on, they were known as Latins, as Juno had requested.

After all his years of wandering and adventure Aeneas was at last able to settle and make a new home. His people built an impressive new city which was called Lavinium after his bride. So Aeneas lived out his days in happiness and contentment, watching his son Ascanius grow to manhood and at last take over the kingdom.

When Aeneas died his mother went to Jupiter with a very special request: she asked if her son could be granted immortality. Jupiter quickly gave his consent, and even Juno did not object. Venus made her way to Lavinium where she commanded the river to purify Aeneas' body, then used her divine powers to make him into a god. The people built a temple in his honour and he was known as Jupiter Indiges or the local Jove.

After the death of his father Ascanius (who was also called Iulus) left Lavinium and founded a new settlement in the hills. This was Alba, the prophesied city of the shining name, and because it was built along a long, hilly ridge it was called Alba Longa. Here the descendants of Aeneas and Ascanius ruled in strength and prosperity for the next four hundred years.

and defenceless, waiting for the final struggle. As he looked despairingly around, he saw a great stone lying nearby and with superhuman strength he managed to lift it to shoulder height, then tried to hurl it at Aeneas. As he struggled to take aim, he began to tremble and stagger helplessly about, his mind and body gripped by an unearthly force. The great stone fell harmlessly and Aeneas, watching for an opportunity from a safe distance, finally hurled his spear. The sharp point burst through Turnus' shield and buried itself deep in his leg. As Turnus fell, a great cry went up from all those who watched, Latins, Rutulians and Trojans alike. Now Aeneas, his sword drawn, stood over his enemy and while Turnus pleaded for mercy,

Romulus and Remus

After many years, the rule of Alba Longa passed to a King called Procas Silvius who had two sons, Numitor and Amulius. Numitor, the elder, was by nature a kind and peace-loving boy whilst his brother Amulius was cruel and ruthless. As the King grew older he began to worry about who would reign when he died.

'My son Numitor ought to rule this kingdom after me,' he thought. 'Custom and the law decree this, and in any case Numitor's gentleness and wisdom will make him a good king. I know Amulius wants my crown and will argue against my decision. He is so headstrong and will stop at nothing to get what he wants. Perhaps if I leave most of my wealth to my younger son that will make him content.'

So Procas left matters. The years passed and eventually the old King died. But his wishes were not fulfilled. Amulius, greedy for power, seized the throne from his brother and took all the riches for himself as well.

The sad and defeated Numitor was driven away from the palace. His brother gave him land outside the city and he settled down to live as a farmer. He had lost his inheritance but he still had health and strength as well as a wife and three young children.

Amulius now had his heart's desire, he was at last King of Alba Longa. Yet he was far from easy in his mind. A persistent fear kept nagging at him. He knew that Numitor would do nothing to take back the crown but he could not be so sure about Numitor's children. When they grew up they would be dangerous.

One violent act led to the next for after careful thought, Amulius could think of only one satisfactory solution. He called his most trusted servants before him and gave them two simple orders. 'Find, and then kill my brother's sons. Do it secretly and with care,' he commanded. 'Then seize his daughter, Rhea Silvia, and bring her to the palace.'

His orders were obeyed. Numitor was grief-stricken. 'My sons are dead,' he cried, 'but spare my daughter. She can do nothing to harm you.'

Tyrant though he was, Amulius felt that to kill Numitor's daughter would be wrong, and he worked out an ingenious plan which would save both Rhea Silvia and his reputation. He arranged for her to be appointed as a priestess of Vesta, the goddess of the sacred fire. This was a great honour. As a Vestal Virgin the girl would enjoy a lifetime of privileged service to the city and the people of Alba Longa. However, like all Vestal Virgins she was forbidden by law to have children. Amulius would be safe.

Of all the gods and goddesses who watched over the affairs of men it was the god Mars who took a particular interest in the fate of Alba Longa. The young King's cruelty and greed made him angry so he decided it was time to interfere.

His first act was to announce his plan to Rhea Silvia in a dream. The dream was vivid and strangely haunting. In it Rhea saw herself wearing a crown of leaves. As she watched, two trees sprouted out from the crown and grew steadily taller until they reached up into the sky. When she awoke, the dream remained vivid to her and all through the day it stayed in her mind. The next night, the dream returned, more real even than before. Seven times she was worried by the same dream and at last she realized its meaning.

'This must be a sign from one of the gods,' she said. 'I'm sure that something very special and unusual is going to happen to me.'

And sure enough it did, for some time later Rhea gave birth to twin boys, the two trees of the dream! There was no hope of concealing the babies from her companions and Rhea knew that she would be punished. The sacred law had been broken and she must die. However, she had hoped and prayed that her two beautiful babies would be spared. She confessed to the high priestess, announcing what she firmly believed, that the father of her sons was the divine Mars. The uproar which followed was tremendous. Rhea was taken before the King immediately. He was astounded and angered by the news. 'Mars indeed!' he shouted in his fury. 'Is this how the gods reward me for my kindness? My family and my kingdom have been dishonoured. Take Rhea Silvia and drown her in the Tiber, and then throw those miserable sons of hers in after her.'

The executioners hurried away to obey the King's orders. Rhea Silvia was thrown roughly into the River Tiber and swept away in its currents. According to legend, however, she did not drown, but was rescued by the river god Tiberinus and made immortal as his wife. The twins were snatched from their mother's arms, then put together into a basket, which, with its screaming contents, was thrown into the dark, swirling waters of the river.

It happened that at the time the Tiber was in full flood and had overflowed its banks. The babies lay helplessly inside the basket as it was swept along and buffeted by the strong currents of the swollen river. Several times it was nearly swamped but at last it reached the calmer water of the shallows at the edge of the flood. There it became entangled in the exposed roots of a large fig tree and was held safely until the flood water went down.

Rhea had been right in thinking that Mars was the father of her twin sons and he continued to look after the abandoned babies. Having saved them from the flood, he now had to find someone to nurse them. One of the creatures sacred to Mars was the wolf and it happened that a great she-wolf lived with her cubs in a near-by cave. As she came down to drink from the river, she heard the desperate cries of the hungry babies and soon found them hidden in the basket. She prised the lid open with her teeth but instead of killing and eating them, as you might expect, she lifted them out and carried them carefully in her mouth back to her cave in the hillside. There she washed them gently with her tongue and fed them with her own milk. Warm and contented, they slept with the cubs, snuggled among the she-wolf's fur.

For a time they lived happily like this but as they grew, the wolf's milk was not enough to keep them alive. They needed more solid food but could not cope with the scraps of meat and bones that the cubs were already learning to gnaw. To save his sons, Mars ordered the birds to feed them and every day the birds of the countryside flew into the cave, carrying bread and wild fruit for the twins. The children grew and were healthy but eventually Mars saw that these wild creatures could not provide for the boys: food and shelter were not enough, they

needed the love and care of other human beings.

Close by the cave lived a herdsman named Faustulus and his wife Laurentia. They were poor people who lived simply and honestly, looking after their master's sheep and goats and growing a few vegetables for the kitchen. They had no children of their own and Mars knew that they would make ideal foster parents for the twins. When the flooded river had subsided, Faustulus had discovered the empty basket beneath the tree. In spite of its journey it looked almost new and he had wondered how it had got there and what it had contained. Later, he noticed birds flying into the cave on the hillside, carrying food in their beaks. Knowing that the cave was the home of a large fierce she-wolf, he was puzzled and for several days he kept a watch on the cave, seeing the birds flying in and out of the entrance and the wolf cubs gambolling among the rocks. Eventually his curiosity overcame his fear. He waited until the wolf left her lair and disappeared among the trees taking her cubs with her. Then he scrambled up to the entrance of the cave, and, glancing back to make sure that the wolf was not returning, he entered.

The cave was chill and eerie. The darkness stood like a wall before him. Straining his ears he heard faint whimpering noises and, feeling his way forward, he discovered the babies. His eyes had become accustomed to the darkness and he could just make out their tiny forms stretched out on a bed of dry grass.

Before he realized what he was doing, he had gathered up the children, one roughly held under each arm, and was running with them outside into the sunlight and fresh air. He only stopped when he approached his hut. His wife stood outside it watching him in astonishment. She thought at first that it was two young goats that her husband carried, but as he drew nearer she clearly saw that they were human babies. Faustulus thrust them into her arms and breathlessly told her the whole strange story. 'These are no ordinary babies,' she said. 'I believe that they are the children of the gods, sent to us to love and cherish. So that's what we must do.'

Together they decided on names for the boys and called them Romulus and Remus. So the strange family began their new life together. The boys grew to be strong, brave young men who helped with the herds and flocks and hunted tirelessly in the surrounding woods.

This peaceful life did not content them for long. They wanted adventure, and found it in the successful game of attacking robbers and brigands who lived in the neighbourhood and stealing the goods *they* had just stolen from someone else. They shared the proceeds of these raids amongst their friends and soon won the support of a large band of young men, all as brave and wild as themselves.

The local brigands, deprived of their normal livelihood, decided that something must be done and planned to catch out the brothers and teach them a lesson. They waited until the day of the festival of Pan and carefully laid their trap. During the feast, when the dancing and drinking was at its height, the brigands attacked. In the fight which followed Remus was taken prisoner. The brigands tied him up securely and took him before King Amulius.
'This man and his brother with their gang of wild thieves have been raiding the land which belongs to Numitor and stealing his cattle,' they declared.

The King had a swift reply, 'Since these ruffians have been raiding my brother's land, he must punish them, not I. Take this man before Numitor. Trouble me no more.'

The unfortunate Remus was dragged away and brought before Numitor. The brigands again made their accusations, explaining that this was only one of two wild brothers, so alike that it was difficult to distinguish between them. Numitor listened but seemed far more interested in gazing at the prisoner's face than in hearing about his crimes. Something about the man standing before him reminded Numitor of his long-lost daughter Rhea and all the painful memories of his earlier life returned. Remembering all his sufferings, he hardly dared to admit the sudden feeling of hope he felt as he looked at Remus.
'I have lost almost everything,' he pondered, 'my throne, my fortune, my sons, my daughter and my grandsons. Why should the gods be kind to me now?' He thought over the facts of the

something to Faustulus, pushing him forward as their spokesman.

As soon as Remus had been carried off by the robbers, Faustulus, who had kept his secret for so long, realized that the truth must be told. Hurriedly he had explained to Romulus all he knew about their origins. Now, reassured by the protection of his two tall foster sons, he began to repeat the story to Numitor. He told of his discovery of the basket by the river, of the cave and then of the young twins in the care of the she-wolf. He went on to tell of the way in which he and his wife had loved and protected the boys and of how they had grown into such noble and fearless young men. Numitor's joy could not be hidden as he looked at the twins.

'I am your grandfather,' Numitor said quietly, hardly able to believe his own words. 'I thought that you were dead, like your mother, but a miracle has kept you alive to bring me joy in my old age. May the gods be praised.'

When Romulus and Remus realized just what their great uncle Amulius had done they became very angry and decided at once that his crimes must be avenged.

The twins knew that they and their small band of followers were no match for the army of Amulius, so that open battle was impossible. A surprise attack on the King himself was the only plan likely to succeed. Their men were divided into several small groups and each group approached the palace from a different direction, coming together at a pre-arranged time, to storm in and surround the King. The brothers drew their swords and approached Amulius, who cowered before them like a cornered animal. Remus spoke first.

'We are the sons of your niece, Rhea Silvia,' he announced, 'and we have come to avenge her death.'

Romulus, angry at the delay, sprang forward and was the first to thrust his sword into the King. Remus followed and the King fell dead at their feet.

Outside, Numitor had gathered the people and the army together. As soon as he saw his grandsons emerge from the palace, their blood-stained swords raised in triumph, he spoke. He told the assembly about the terrible crimes of

case. 'These men say that you have a twin brother. Is it true?' asked Numitor.
'Yes, my lord,' answered Remus.

Again Numitor was lost in thought. 'They are certainly the right age,' he said to himself. 'Could they really be Rhea's children, my own grandsons?' The possibility frightened him. If it were true, the great gods themselves must be involved.
'I wish to be left alone with this man,' ordered Numitor. 'Leave us.'

As everyone hurried from the room there was a great noise of shouting in the courtyard outside and two men thrust themselves past the guards at the door. Numitor saw an old peasant and a strong young man, the image of the prisoner. It was Faustulus and Romulus who had come to save Remus. Now all three stood before the astonished Numitor. Romulus bent to whisper

So far the brothers were in agreement and plans went ahead smoothly, but inevitably the brothers disagreed about which of them was to rule the new city. Since they were twins neither was the senior. Both wanted to be King and to call the new city after himself.

Eventually, after a great deal of arguing, they agreed to let the gods decide the matter. In those days, people believed that the gods showed their decisions through signs of nature. Having together put their question to the gods at a temple in the city of Alba, the brothers took up their positions, Romulus on the hill called the Palatine and Remus on a neighbouring hill called the Aventine. There they waited.

Remus was the first to see something which could be taken as a sign: six vultures flew together across the sky. So many of these usually solitary birds flying together was a very unusual sight and vultures were also thought to be especially sacred to the gods. The event was taken to mean that Remus was the chosen King and the matter seemed to be settled when Romulus returned to announce that he had seen no less than twelve vultures flying together above the Palatine Hill.

Now the people began to take sides, the supporters of Remus proclaiming him King because he had been the first to see a sign, the supporters of Romulus proclaiming him King because he had seen more vultures than his brother. Stirred by feelings of jealousy and ambition, the twins soon began to argue and then to fight. Romulus, certain that he would be the new King, started to build a wall round his settlement on the Palatine Hill. Remus, mocking his brother's efforts, was foolish enough to jump over the wall, to prove how easily he could overcome it.

This jeering maddened Romulus so much that he flew into a terrible rage and killed his brother. Standing triumphantly over Remus' body, he shouted a warning to anyone who might challenge him: 'The same fate awaits anyone else who dares to leap over my wall.'

All the people who had left Alba with the twins now proclaimed Romulus King and the new city being built on the Palatine Hill was called Rome, after its illustrious founder.

Amulius; about the birth of Romulus and Remus and the way in which the gods had protected them; and lastly about the well-deserved death of the King. Above the murmur of the crowd came the clear voices of the two brothers, boldly proclaiming Numitor as the rightful King of Alba. Their shouts were taken up by the people.
'Numitor is our King!'
'Long live King Numitor!'

Numitor was welcomed into the royal palace by his subjects and so began his happy and peaceful reign. Romulus and Remus served under their grandfather for several years but they longed for more power. Eventually their chance came, for Alba was becoming overcrowded and a new city was badly needed. It was decided that Romulus and Remus should start a new settlement and where better than the place where the twins had been left to die as babies and where they had grown to manhood?

The Sabine women

The new city of Rome began to grow. Romulus was ambitious and made the area of the city very large, too large in fact for the number of people living there. The problem was how to attract more people to fill the city. Romulus decided to follow the ancient practice of making his city a place of refuge. Soon, an assortment of people flocked in from many miles around, all eager for somewhere to live. Among them were slaves who had escaped from their masters, criminals, homeless and destitute people; all people who were unwelcome in any other place.

Romulus, however, was delighted with them. He had appointed a hundred men to be the 'City Fathers' or Senate and these he called together.

'Rome is now strong,' he said. 'No city will dare to challenge us, but we must think of the future. We all know that we need more women. Most of the men here have no wives. How can we find women for the men to marry?'

After a long discussion it was agreed to send envoys to neighbouring cities in order to arrange alliances and inter-marriages.

When the envoys returned each had the same reply: no-one wanted to have anything to do with the Romans. The idea of their young women marrying a mob of slaves, criminals and vagrants was quite unthinkable. The men of Rome felt insulted and wanted to take up arms immediately. Romulus had to prevent an open fight; besides, he had a much better idea.

Preparations were well under way for the summer festival of the Consualia in honour of the god Consus. It was decided to make the event really elaborate and to invite everyone, from far and wide, to join in the celebrations. On the day of the festival people crowded into Rome, intent on enjoying a good day out. Apart from anything else they probably wanted to see the new city and study its defences. There were people from places near to Rome such as Caenina, Crustumium and Antemnae but most numerous were the Sabines, Rome's most powerful neighbours. Men, women and children thronged the open areas and public buildings within the city and once the formal religious rites had been completed they made their way to the place where the chariot races were held. Although Consus was a

87

god of the crops, he was particularly associated with horses and for that reason all the horses and mules were garlanded and crowned with flowers. An atmosphere of good-humoured expectation filled the city.

The show began and the moment for which the Romans were waiting arrived. As Romulus stood up and gave an agreed signal, groups of men moved in among the spectators and seized all the young women they could see. Panic spread among the crowd. The girls cried out in fear and tried their best to escape, but it was useless to struggle. They were carried swiftly to places of safety within the city, leaving their parents, brothers and friends standing helplessly by.

The visitors had been deceived and insulted and as they hurried back home they angrily voiced their feelings. To have their womenfolk captured in war was one thing, but to have them snatched away during a religious festival was terrible. Romulus and his accomplices would surely be punished by the gods for their crime.

The young women, too, were very unhappy about what had happened. Romulus visited each in turn, reassuring them.
'If only your parents had listened to our envoys,' he said. 'But you have nothing to fear. As married women, you can share in the future greatness of the city and enjoy the privileges of being its citizens. Besides, you will feel differently once you have children at your sides. You may be angry now but love will soon follow.'

He had advice for the men as well. They should be loving husbands, he told them, and work hard to make good homes for their new wives. The men helped by flattering the women and soon their anger cooled and disappeared.

Although the women settled down and accepted what had happened to them, their parents and relatives remained very angry. Since the gods apparently refused to punish the Romans for their crime, they all appealed to the Sabine King, Tatius, to take matters into his own hands. The King was not eager to go to war over a few girls and for a time he did nothing. However, the people from the cities of Caenina, Crustumium and Antemnae, who had also lost their young women, grew impatient at the delay and organized their own attacks on Rome.

The army from Caenina attacked first but was quickly defeated by a Roman force led by Romulus himself. Not content with their victory, they marched on the enemy city and captured it. Romulus himself slew the King, stripped him of his armour and returned to Rome to celebrate his victory. He took the armour to the Capitol Hill and offered it to Jupiter at the god's sacred oak tree. He then arranged for a temple to be built on the site, the first temple in the city, in honour of Jupiter.

The defeat of Caenina did not dampen the spirits of the armies of Antemnae and Crustumium. They, too, attacked Roman territory and they, too, were soon defeated and their cities taken. It was then that Hersilie, the wife of Romulus, made a suggestion.
'Why don't you issue pardons to the people of the three cities you have captured and then invite the parents of the girls to come and live in Rome?'

Romulus welcomed the idea and the people of the conquered cities were also in favour. Parents and relatives of the women moved into the city of Rome and people from Rome moved out to settle on the rich farming land in the captured areas. In this way the bonds between the different cities were strengthened and Rome's sphere of influence became wider.

All this time the Sabines had been ominously silent and the Romans believed that they were planning an attack of their own. They were right, for by that time the Sabine King had realized that Rome must be subdued before it became too strong. His plan was to capture the stronghold which Romulus had built just outside the city, then launch his main attack from there. The stronghold was commanded by Spurius Tarpeius who had a young daughter called Tarpeia. Tarpeia happened to be outside the walls of the fortress one day drawing water when she heard someone calling her name from among the trees nearby. She saw the glint of jewels among the branches and went to see what it was, for she loved jewels, gold and silver, above anything else. Among the trees she found the Sabine King surrounded by a troop of his soldiers, all fully armed and wearing, as was their custom, heavy gold bracelets and jewelled rings. She showed no fear but went closer to the men, fascinated by their finery. Then the King spoke.

'Fair Tarpeia,' he said, 'I will come straight to the point. If you will open the gate of the fortress tonight so that we can enter, we will give you anything that you desire.'

Tarpeia considered this for a while, gazing all the time at the gold and jewels. Then she replied, 'I will open the gate for you if you will give me those things which you wear on your arms.'

'We will gladly give them to you,' answered the King, 'once we are inside the fortress.'

Tarpeia was well satisfied and could hardly wait until darkness came and she was able to creep down to the little gate in the fortress wall where the Sabines waited. Once inside, the King whispered to Tarpeia, 'Now your reward. What did we promise?'

The girl was by this time regretting what she had done for enemy soldiers were all about her and she felt threatened and afraid.

'You promised to give me those things on your arms,' she said, hoping that her voice did not betray her fear.

'Then you shall have your desire,' mumbled the King as he removed first his heavy shield, then his gold bracelets. He threw them at the girl's feet and she cried out in surprise. The soldiers followed his example, so that soon the terrified girl was surrounded by shields and heavy bracelets. Still the soldiers did not stop.

'That is payment enough!' she sobbed, as shield after shield crashed on top of her, crushing her to death under their weight.

The men solemnly retrieved their gold armbands and their mighty shields ready for action, then took the body of Tarpeia and threw it from the top of the rock on which the fortress had been built.

'That's what we think of traitors,' said the King harshly.

Having taken possession of the stronghold, the Sabines prepared their attack on the city itself. Romulus had gathered his troops in full force and now moved forward towards the enemy. The Sabines advanced down the hill to meet them and the battle began. Both sides fought bravely but the Sabines had the advantage and drove the Romans back in disorder towards their own defences. The situation was desperate. Romulus looked about him, then raised his sword high in the air and shouted above the din of battle:

'Hear me, mighty Jupiter, Father of gods and men. Your city is threatened. The Sabines are pressing in on every side. Remove fear from Roman hearts and grant that we may defend this place. I will build a temple here to remind men in days to come that you helped Rome in her hour of need.' Then he called to his men. 'Jupiter is with us. Fight on brave Romans!'

Miraculously their courage and strength returned.

The Sabines were led by a man called Mettius Curtius who was so confident of victory that he

streaming out behind them, their clothes billowing in the wind as they ran. Ignoring the flying spears and clashing swords, they pushed themselves in a great crowd between the two armies. Looking towards their fathers on one side, their husbands on the other, they appealed for peace.

'You are fighting because of us,' they cried, 'but we don't want to be left without husbands or fathers. We would rather die ourselves.'

Silence fell on the battlefield. For a time no-one moved, then the commanders of the two armies put away their weapons at the same moment and made peace with one another. Immediately soldiers on both sides joined hands in friendship.

Peace returned and the two nations lived as one under the joint rule of their two Kings. Eventually the Sabine King, Tatius, died, leaving Romulus to rule alone. It was then that Mars, the father of Romulus, persuaded Jupiter to allow his son a place among the gods.

While Jupiter stirred up a sudden, ferocious storm, Mars raced off to Rome in his winged chariot. He found Romulus seated before his people on the Palatine Hill and swooped down, making Romulus disappear into thin air as he descended. In place of the human Romulus his god-likeness appeared but then that, too, vanished, leaving the frightened spectators to wonder at the strange happening. Then, realizing that Romulus had left them forever, they began to build a temple in honour of their dead King, the founder of Rome, and to worship him under a new name as the god Quirinus.

Poor Hersilie, the wife of Romulus, was heart-broken at the loss of her husband and was constantly to be found at his temple weeping. Juno felt great pity for her and one day, while Hersilie stood praying in the temple, the goddess caused a star to fall to the ground beside her. Immediately Hersilie's hair flamed around her head and she ascended with the star to be reunited with her husband. Both were overjoyed. The newly-appointed god embraced his wife and in so doing changed both her appearance and her name. Together, as Quirinus and Hora, they lived in heavenly bliss and looked down forever on their city of Rome.

began boasting loudly of what he would do once they had taken the city. He was in the middle of describing his triumphant entry when Romulus led a fierce counter-attack, taking the Sabines completely by surprise. Mettius' horse, startled by the sudden noise and confusion, bolted, with its rider still clinging to its back. The horse, quite out of control, plunged into marshy land close to the river and the fighting stopped while everyone stood watching Mettius and his horse struggling helplessly, sinking deeper and deeper into the mire. Mettius managed to disentangle himself from the harness just as the horse was sucked below the surface. A cheer went up from his men as he made his way to the safety of dry land but the incident had destroyed their will to fight and the Romans were now able to drive them back with ease.

All this time the captured Sabine women had stood watching the battle which was being fought because of them. As they saw more and more men falling dead or wounded, they could endure it no longer and they rushed onto the battlefield, their children in their arms, their hair

Numa, the wise King

The sudden disappearance of Romulus left the people of Rome with a problem, for there was no-one suitable to take his place as King. The Sabines wanted one of their people to be the next King for they were afraid that their Roman allies would become too strong. The Romans, of course, wanted a King from their own people and hated the thought of being ruled by a Sabine.

While the quarrel continued many of the neighbouring cities were collecting their armies together ready to attack Roman territory. The men of the Senate saw the danger and decided to ask the people to elect a King. When the citizens were assembled, a leading senator addressed them:

'People of Rome, Sabines and Romans alike, you are free to choose a King. If the man you decide on is worthy to succeed Romulus, then the Senate will confirm your choice. May good luck and the blessing of the gods be with you.'

The people were delighted at the idea of choosing their leader for themselves and the search for the right man began. Despite all their enquiries only one suitable candidate for the throne could be found. His name was Numa Pompilius, a Sabine from the town of Cures, a man with a great reputation for wisdom and goodness. He had spent many years studying the ways of nature and the movement of the stars. He had prayed to the gods constantly and had learned their laws. He knew and loved the blessings of peace and harmony.

When he was asked if he would consider becoming the next King of Rome he was surprised and reluctant.

'Kings are men of war,' he said. 'They command great armies. I am a man of peace. You all know that.'

They tried to persuade him by telling him that Rome needed peace. 'Become King,' they said, 'and you can bring peace to the land. No-one but you can do that.'

Eventually Numa's name was put before the Senate and everyone agreed that he should be the next King. When Numa himself arrived in Rome he asked the Senate if the gods could be consulted to make quite sure that they, too, agreed with the choice. An augur, a man who could interpret signs from the gods, was appointed and he went with Numa to the top of the Capitol Hill to observe the sky. There the augur prayed to the Father of Heaven. 'Great Jupiter, if it is your wish that this man, Numa Pompilius, should be King of Rome, show us your sign in the sky above.'

The augur suggested what the sign should be and the two men waited, watching the sky for any unusual sight. Eventually the sign appeared, just as the augur had described it: a flock of vultures flew slowly overhead, their great wings spread wide to ride the currents of air high above. It was the same sign that Romulus had seen all those years before and seemed a clear indication that Jupiter approved the peoples' choice. Numa, accepting the will of the gods at last, descended from the hill and was crowned King of Rome.

His reign of peace began but progress was slow, for everyone was accustomed to fighting and it was not easy to persuade them to lay down their swords. The first thing that Numa did was to have a temple built for Janus, the god of gates and doors and also of beginnings. The temple had two huge doors and these were used to show whether Rome was at war or at peace. When they were open everyone knew that a war was in progress and when they were closed, that war had ceased. After making treaties of friendship with all the neighbouring cities, Numa ordered the gates of Janus' temple to be firmly closed and they remained shut throughout his long reign.

Numa saw his next task very clearly. Without wars to fight, his people were likely to become lazy and troublesome so he had to teach them how to make the most of peace. He had found great comfort and joy himself in serving the gods so he taught the people to do the same. Numa was married, but his wife was no ordinary mortal. She was the water-nymph Egeria who lived just outside the city by a spring of pure water. This spring was surrounded by a sacred grove which few were allowed to enter and there Egeria held long conversations with the Muses, the nine daughters of Jupiter who were in charge of literature and the arts—all the pastimes of peace. Egeria passed on what she learned to her husband and he in turn instructed his people. Knowing that they were being taught by the gods, the people accepted Numa's changes to their way of life more readily.

One of the important things that he did was to introduce the calendar. He divided the year into twelve months and decided on the times when the different gods and goddesses should be worshipped. Then he appointed priests to take charge of the religious ceremonies, especially those concerned with the worship of Jupiter, Mars and Quirinus. He also appointed priestesses to serve the hearth-goddess Vesta at her temple in the city.

Numa was really a priest as well as a King but he realized that not all the kings that followed him would be able to fulfil both functions. Most, he thought, would be away from Rome much of the time fighting wars. He therefore appointed a man called the pontifex, or priest, to be responsible in the King's place for all religious matters. This idea was a good one and the pontifex remained as a position of importance in Rome for hundreds of years.

With Numa as their King the people of Rome were always fully occupied, making sure that the ceremonies in honour of the gods and goddesses were performed correctly and that the whole community was run according to divine laws. Gradually people in the neighbouring cities looked to Rome not as a military camp, but as a holy community in which the gods were more important than anything else. No-one dreamed of attacking such a place, for to do so would have been an offence against the gods.

Numa was King for more than forty years, but gradually his strength failed and he died. Because he had been concerned with peace rather than with power everyone thought of him with great affection. He had been a father to them as well as a King, and the Roman people had learned much from his example. His death was mourned by all, but no-one missed him more than his wife, the nymph Egeria. She left her sacred grotto near the city and fled to Aricia, in the mountains south of Rome. There, in the woods on the shore of a lake, she hid herself in the grove of the goddess Diana.

Nothing could console Egeria for the loss of her husband and she wept without ceasing. Eventually the noise of her grief became so loud and persistent that it interrupted the worship of the goddess. The nymphs of the sacred grove

gathered round her and implored her to stop weeping but still she sobbed uncontrollably. Then Diana herself took charge and sent her companion Virbius to console her. Virbius was, like Diana herself, a deity of the forest and of hunting, and to divert the nymph's attention from her sorrow he told her of his own unhappy life.

'My name was once Hippolytus,' he began. 'I am the son of Theseus king of Athens and Hippolyte, Queen of the Amazons. I was wronged by my father and stepmother and sent into exile, but as I drove my chariot away from Athens along the coast road, Neptune the sea-god caused a monster to rise suddenly out of the waves to block the road. My horses were frightened and went wildly out of control. My chariot was smashed and I was flung out, then dragged helplessly along by the fleeing horses, entangled in the reins. I died there at the roadside and was already entering the kingdom of Pluto when the doctor Aesculapius, using his powerful herbal remedies, restored me to life. 'Then Diana came to my rescue and hid me in a mist so that she could work a new miracle. She completely changed my appearance so that no-one could recognize me, for many of the gods

were angry because I had cheated death. Aesculapius was not so fortunate. Jupiter would not allow a mere mortal to have so much power, so he killed the good physician with a thunderbolt. Diana brought me here to her sanctuary and re-named me Virbius. I have lived here happily ever since, pleased to serve my mistress.'

Egeria listened quietly to this amazing story but as soon as it was finished she began weeping afresh, apparently more upset than ever. She lay there on the grass, her body shaking with sobs, her tears pouring endlessly into the ground. Diana, who was goddess of springs and streams as well as of the woods, was moved by the nymph's devotion to her dead husband. 'Weep on, Egeria,' she said kindly, 'for grief like yours can know no end.' Then, with a wave of her hand, she transformed Egeria's body into a spring which bubbled up from the grass and began to fill a rocky hollow with cool, clear water.

From that day on, the spring in the sacred grove of Diana at Aricia was known as the Spring of Egeria and pilgrims from all over Italy worshipped the faithful nymph there for many years afterwards.

The house of Tarquin

The next King to reign after Numa was Tullus Hostilius. He was a soldier and, unlike Numa, longed for the adventures of war. Once King, he found the slightest excuse to start fighting. His first victims were the people of Alba Longa, the city which Ascanius, Aeneas' son, had founded long years before. The fact that the people of Alba were closely related to his own Romans did not seem to bother him and he defeated them easily, forcing them to leave their city and to settle in Rome. Soldiers moved into Alba Longa to carry out the King's orders and the people stood watching them, too upset to speak or to try to stop them. They emerged sadly from their homes, carrying just a few possessions for the journey, and were herded together on the road leading out of the city. At once the soldiers began to destroy all the buildings, leaving only the temples intact. The people of Alba looked back towards the city they loved so much to see only clouds of dust rising into the sky. It seemed that their gods had deserted them.

Tullus was pleased with his success and promptly declared war on other neighbouring cities, defeating them all and adding greatly to the wealth and power of Rome. It was then that a strange event took place. It was reported in Rome that stones had been seen raining down on the hill where the city of Alba once stood. A group of Albans was sent to investigate and, sure enough, they found a storm of stones falling from the sky and rattling in a thick layer to the ground. As they stood cowering they heard a voice speaking stern words of warning:

'Albans, you have deserted the religion of your ancestors. You do this at your peril. Return to the worship of your gods.'

It was a timely warning. Back in Rome the soothsayers were consulted and on their advice a nine-day festival was held so that Albans and Romans alike could renew their acquaintance with their gods.

In spite of this warning, King Tullus was still eager for further warfare. He hated to see his young men idling away their time at home when they could be out on the battlefield. Before he could march out again, however, Rome was afflicted by a terrible plague. Even Tullus became ill and in his weakness he forgot his war plans.

He even turned to religion and joined his people in praying for the health of the city and a return to peace. Perhaps he was trying to be like Numa, for one day he was reading through the books that Numa had written when he found the description of a secret rite honouring Jupiter. Without telling anyone he carried out the rite, probably hoping to receive the god's blessing and guidance. However, he made a serious mistake in the way he performed the ceremony and Jupiter, angered by his carelessness, sent a bolt of lightning to strike the royal palace. Flames leaped through the King's apartment, trapping Tullus and burning him alive.

After Tullus' death a new King was elected. He was Ancus Marcius, a descendant of the wise King Numa. He would certainly have followed Numa's example of peace and holiness if Rome had not been attacked by the people of Latium, who wished to test the new king's strength. Although Ancus wanted peace, he saw that in this case it would be impossible without sacrificing Rome's honour. However, he believed that religion and war could go together; the gods should not be forgotten. Under his leadership the war against the Latins was successful and again the population and size of Rome grew.

It was during the reign of Ancus that a man of wealth and ambition called Lucumo moved to Rome. He came from the Etruscan town of Tarquinii with his wife Tanaquil and his two sons. It was Tanaquil who had realized the opportunities which Rome offered and who had persuaded her husband to make the move. As they neared the city in their fine carriage an eagle swooped suddenly down from the clear sky, snatched off Lucumo's cap and flew away with it, only to return immediately and replace it neatly on the astonished man's head. Tanaquil was overjoyed.

'You realize what this means?' she cried. 'You are going to be a great man. This sign from heaven shows that you will one day be crowned king. This is even more than I had hoped for.'

Once in Rome they bought a large house in the wealthy quarter of the city and began to gain a reputation as prosperous but friendly foreigners. Lucumo changed his name to Lucius

Tarquinius Priscus and soon became known simply as Tarquin. He entertained on a lavish scale and made many influential friends, among them the King himself. Skilfully, Tarquin took advantage of his friendship with the King, so that eventually Ancus relied on him entirely for help and advice. He even made Tarquin the guardian of his two young sons.

By this time Ancus was growing old and it was generally thought that one of his sons would succeed him. When he died, however, Tarquin seized his opportunity. He sent the princes away on a hunting expedition, then called a meeting of the people. In a rousing speech he told everyone of his own virtues and of his willingness to become King. Convinced by his words, they voted overwhelmingly in his favour and by the time the princes returned Tarquin was firmly established as Rome's new King. The boys were forced to accept the will of the people but they never forgave him for the trick he had played.

Tarquin's first act as King was to re-start the war against the Latins. The campaign was a success and on his return to Rome Tarquin celebrated his victory with elaborate and impressive public games. More wars followed and many cities and large areas of land were captured. The power of Rome grew rapidly during the reign of this ambitious King, but he was not concerned only with war. He made useful changes in the army and in the way Rome was governed and he organized the building of defensive walls and great sewers. He also laid the foundations of a temple of Jupiter on the Capitol Hill.

Among those living at the palace during Tarquin's rule was the queen of one of the Latin cities which Tarquin had captured and her young son Servius Tullius. The child was lying asleep one day when, suddenly, flames appeared all around his head. There were many people nearby and when they saw it they called out in alarm. The disturbance brought Tarquin and his wife Tanaquil hurrying to the cradle. Tanaquil understood the meaning of such heavenly signs and she told everyone to be quiet and not to disturb the sleeping child. In a short while the boy awoke and the fire disappeared, leaving no trace of where it had been.

97

Queen Tanaquil spoke to her husband later when they were alone.

'That child,' she said, 'is destined to become great and to bring glory to our family and to Rome. From now on we must see that he is properly cared for.'

The boy was treated like a prince of the house of Tarquin and as he grew everyone came to love and respect him. The King saw that Servius would be a perfect son-in-law and he made sure that he married his daughter. It seemed certain that the young Servius would be the next king.

The two sons of Ancus, however, still felt very bitter about the way Tarquin had deceived them and when they realized that Servius was likely to inherit the throne and deprive them of power once again, they decided to act. Their plan was a desperate one: they plotted to murder Tarquin.

The sons employed two rough shepherds to carry out their plan. The shepherds pretended to fight each other just outside the palace and they were taken before the King so that he could

settle the dispute. While Tarquin was listening to one of them, the other crept round and attacked him from behind with a dagger, seriously wounding him. A tremendous uproar followed. The shepherds were caught trying to escape and an angry crowd of onlookers soon gathered outside the palace.

Queen Tanaquil tried in vain to save Tarquin's life, using all the skills she knew to heal his wound. Then, seeing that it was hopeless, she sent for Servius, showed him the dying king and spoke quietly to him.

'Now is your chance. The throne is yours if you act quickly. The gods themselves wish you to be king; remember the ring of heavenly fire which flickered around your head so long ago. Be the man I know that you are.'

The crowd outside had grown rapidly so, to give Servius more time, Tanaquil stood at an upstairs window and called down to them. She told them that the King was not badly hurt and would recover soon.

'In the meantime,' she said, 'follow Servius, for he will act in the King's place until he is better.'

Of course, the King never did recover and Servius took the throne without difficulty. So his long and successful reign began, but there were jealous people in his own household who for years schemed and plotted in order to gain power for themselves. Chief among them was Tarquin's son, also called Tarquin, and his wife, Servius' own daughter Tullia. Their ambition was boundless. Each had committed murder in order to become man and wife, and by further scheming and plotting they moved closer to grasping the throne. Tullia constantly taunted Tarquin, spurring him to action. Eventually, by bribing and persuading many of the influential families of Rome, he gained the support he needed. Speaking as if he was already King, he

summoned a meeting of the Senate and in a fiery speech he blackened the name of Servius.

Meanwhile, Servius had been told what was happening and he stormed angrily into the meeting and shouted at Tarquin.
'What are you doing, Tarquin? By what right do you summon the Senate and sit in my royal chair?'
'Because I am a King's son,' was the reply, 'which is more than you are. The throne is mine by right of birth.'

Everyone began to shout at once as the senators supported the rival claims. As the noise grew louder, news of the uproar spread through the city and an excited mob outside began to batter at the door, demanding entry. Seeing his chance of the throne disappearing, Tarquin rushed at the old King, lifted him bodily in the air, then carried him outside and flung him down the steps of the Senate House. The crowd drew back as Servius struggled to his feet but a group of Tarquin's supporters surrounded him and dragged him off to murder him, leaving his body lying in the street.

At that moment Tullia arrived and summoned her husband from the Senate House to address the mob. She was the first to proclaim him King and, urged on by his supporters, the people soon took up the cry. Then she sprang exultantly into her chariot and was driven away at full gallop towards her house. As they rounded the corner, the charioteer pulled up suddenly and pointed to the body of the dead King lying abandoned in the road ahead.
'Drive on,' cried Tullia, scarcely giving the body a second glance in her triumph. As the chariot drove over her father's body, blood spattered up, marking the wheels and staining Tullia's clothes with red.

Thus began the reign of Rome's last King.

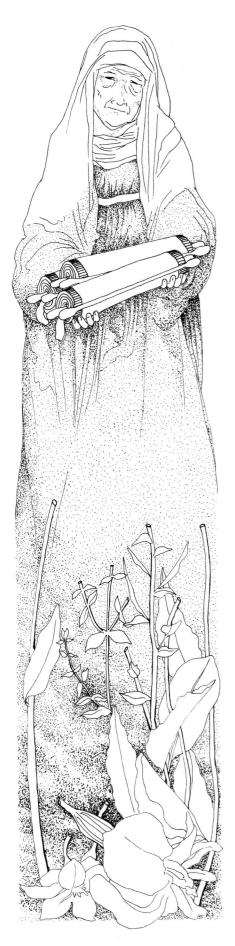

Tarquin the Proud

Rome's new King called himself Tarquinius Superbus or, in other words, Tarquin the Proud. Certainly his actions made that name very suitable. He had taken the throne by force and he had to keep it by force. He had no real right to be King because he had not been elected, and there were many in the Senate who were against him because of the violent way in which he had taken power for himself. Senators who spoke out against him were quickly executed, and before long the others feared him too much to say anything. In fact the only way in which he could rule was to make everyone fear him. His victims were either killed or sent into exile, leaving all their possessions to add to Tarquin's wealth. He made so many enemies that before long he had to have a strong bodyguard to protect him wherever he went.

Tarquin and Tullia had three sons. The youngest of them was called Sextus, a man who was as violent and cruel as his parents. With the help of this son Tarquin fought and won many battles against neighbouring cities. However, there was one place, a city called Gabii, which was stronger than the rest and would never submit to the rule of Rome. Tarquin tried everything to conquer it but eventually had to leave Gabii and take his army back to Rome. There he and Sextus thought of a devious way to defeat the stubborn city.

One day Sextus staggered towards the gates of Gabii, smeared with blood and with his clothes dirty and torn. He was allowed in and told his story to the city elders. 'The king, my father, has turned his cruelty against his own family,' explained Sextus. 'No-one is safe. I only just managed to escape, but his soldiers have been hunting for me with orders to kill me.'

So he continued, making up a great many details to convince them that he was speaking the truth. Then he told them of his plan to gather an army strong enough to march against Tarquin and the insolent Romans.

The people of Gabii did not turn Sextus away. Gradually they came to trust him and take to heart the advice that he gave them. Eventually he was given command of the army and worked hard to win the admiration of the soldiers. With the first part of his mission accomplished, he sent a messenger secretly to Tarquin asking what he should do next.

The messenger spoke in private to the King, reporting what Sextus had said and asking for a reply. Tarquin walked silently up and down the room deep in thought, but said nothing. Then he made his way into the palace garden, with the messenger close behind, anxious to have the King's answer. The garden was bright with flowers and as the King walked among them he took his stick and deliberately struck off the heads of the tallest blooms.

'Sire, what reply shall I give to your son?' asked the messenger again.

The King merely turned and wandered away into the palace. On his return to Sextus the puzzled messenger recounted what had happened. Sextus understood at once what his father intended and set about destroying all Gabii's most influential citizens. He arranged for them to be brought to trial on various trumped-up charges and then executed or, if that was impossible, he had them murdered in secret. In this way Sextus and his supporters gained control of the city and Tarquin added Gabii to his conquests without even leaving Rome.

Tarquin now began to think about his future reputation. He wanted men to remember the greatness of his family for ever, so he turned his attention to building. He decided to complete the temple of Jupiter which his father had begun on the Capitol Hill and as he wanted it to be a really splendid building, he employed expert Etruscan craftsmen and engineers to work on it. The city's poor were used as labourers. When the temple was finished he began other ambitious projects, among them the building of a giant amphitheatre. While everyone had been happy to help in the building of the temple, they felt differently about the other work which they were forced to do and a feeling of discontent spread among the people.

It was not long after this that Tarquin was visited by a wizened old woman who had with her nine very ancient books. She spread the books out before the King. 'These books,' she explained, 'will be of great use to you and to all those who come after you for they contain clues to the whole future history of your race.'

The King did not believe it. He wanted to look at the books for himself to make sure that the old woman was telling the truth but she drew back, hiding them under her cloak.

'No,' she said, 'first you must pay me for the books. I cannot show them to you until then.'

'What is their price?' asked Tarquin.

The woman named a very large sum of money, so large that the King laughed in her face.

'I could ransom a king with that,' he told her. 'Be off with you and take your books with you.'

The next day she returned to the palace and demanded to speak to Tarquin. This time she had only six books to sell. The other three she had burned.

'I suppose you still want me to buy your books. What is the price of the six that remain? I'm not interested unless they are much cheaper than they were yesterday.'

The old woman asked the same price as before.

'What!' cried the King. 'This is absurd. Stop wasting my time.'

Angrily, he ordered the old woman to leave and she walked calmly away, taking the six books with her. Although Tarquin had dismissed her in a rage, he continued to worry about what had happened. The old woman kept returning to his thoughts and, wondering if perhaps he had been too hasty, he decided to seek the advice of his priests. When they had heard all the details, they told him, 'From what you have described, she must be a Sibyl, one of the wise women chosen by the gods to pass on their words to humankind. If she was a Sibyl her books are beyond price. If only we had known of this sooner. If she returns again, we beg you to buy the books whatever the cost.'

On the following day the Sibyl did come back, but she carried only three books, having burned the other three.

'Well, will you buy the three books that remain?' she asked when the King greeted her.

'What is your price, old woman?' replied Tarquin.

The amount was the same as before but this time Tarquin gladly paid it and took the books reverently from her. She left Rome and was never seen there again. The books, known from that day as the Sibylline Books, were kept in a vault beneath Tarquin's newly built temple on the Capitol Hill and only consulted when Rome was threatened by serious troubles.

If Tarquin had been worried by the strange events surrounding his purchase of the sacred books he was even more worried by the appearance of a snake in the palace. The creature slithered out from a crack in a wooden pillar and seemed quite unaffected by the people around it. Tarquin was among the first to see the snake as it wriggled silently across the floor and he was suddenly afraid, for its appearance was a very bad omen. His wise men and soothsayers were called together but they could not agree on what it meant. In the end Tarquin decided to consult the world's most famous oracle, at Delphi in Greece. As he was afraid to leave Rome himself he decided to send the only two people he could really trust, his two sons Titus and Arruns.

They left immediately on the long and dangerous journey, taking with them their cousin Brutus, a young man who was destined to surprise them all. Brutus was the son of Tarquin's sister and everyone thought of him as being a half-wit. However, Brutus was anything but half-witted. His apparent stupidity was simply his own clever disguise, designed to save him from the cruelty of his uncle. Tarquin lived in constant fear of everyone around him but especially of members of his own family who, he suspected, were all plotting to kill him and take his throne. He had arranged for the murder of any number of them but thinking Brutus to be a harmless simpleton, he had only taken the young man's property and left him alive as an amusing companion for his sons.

In due course the three men reached Delphi and consulted the oracle as the King had instructed. Before returning home the two brothers could not resist asking one further question.
'Which of us will be the next King of Rome?' asked the older brother.

There was a pause. Then came the voice of

Apollo's priestess in reply: 'He who shall be the first to kiss his mother shall rule Rome.'

Eagerly the brothers prepared to leave for home. Each, of course, wanted to be the first to greet his mother. Only Brutus realized the truth hidden in the words of the oracle and as he moved away from the shrine he pretended to trip, falling forward on to his face so that his lips touched the Earth, the true mother of all.

When they returned to Rome they found everyone hastily preparing for war. Tarquin had decided that more money was needed to pay for all his ambitious building projects, so he had declared war on the wealthiest of his neighbouring cities, Ardea. The city defences were stronger than Tarquin had suspected and easily withstood the attacks of his army, but he persisted, knowing that he would win in the end. He prepared his men for a long seige.

Meanwhile, Brutus decided that it was time to act. The people had tolerated the cruelty of the Tarquins for long enough and their enemies in the city were ready to rise up and destroy them. His visit to Delphi had given Brutus new confidence and he stopped acting the half-wit. Instead, while the King and his sons were away besieging Ardea, he gathered a strong band of loyal subjects ready for action. Popular support for Brutus soon spread among the common people of Rome and before long the whole city was demanding an immediate end to Tarquin's tyrannical rule. The Queen, Tullia, fled from the palace, was hounded by the mob and eventually escaped from the city. When the news of the uprising reached Tarquin he hurried back to Rome with his sons, only to find the gates closed against him. Brutus, meanwhile, had travelled to Ardea and persuaded both the Ardeans and the Roman army to support him. Tarquin and his sons were sent away from Rome to spend the rest of their days as exiles.

Brutus was enthusiastically acclaimed as 'the Liberator' but he did not become King, for the rule of Kings was over in Rome. The city became a republic and was ruled by two magistrates called consuls who were elected afresh each year. In the first year of the new Roman Republic one of the consuls was, of course, Brutus the Liberator.

The early Republic

Not everyone in Rome was happy with the rule of the new consuls. Some preferred the old system of kingship and there was in particular a group of young men who wanted Tarquin to return to the throne. One day while these young men were making their plans a slave overheard the conversation and reported them to Brutus, who immediately had them arrested. Among the plotters were his own two sons.

At the trial which followed Brutus longed to use his power to save his sons, but he realized that this was impossible. The people looked to him to set a good example and he must put his duty to Rome above everything else. His sons were guilty and, sadly, he ordered them to be executed with the others. In so doing he gained the respect of all the people.

When Tarquin heard that the plot had been discovered he was both disappointed and angry. He desperately wanted to regain power in Rome, and since cunning had not succeeded, he decided to use force. He persuaded two Etruscan cities to support him and with his new army he marched on Rome. The battle raged for a whole day, during which one of Tarquin's sons and the consul Brutus were killed. During the night which followed the Etruscan army was woken from sleep by a great voice, speaking from the depths of a nearby wood. 'Listen Etruscans,' it said. 'Listen Tarquin. I, Silvanus, give you this warning. It is useless to go on fighting, for the Romans have already won. Go home now while you still can.'

The Etruscans were so afraid that they packed their belongings at once, although it was the middle of the night, and immediately left the field of battle. The next day the Romans returned home to celebrate the victory.

Tarquin was not deterred for long by his defeat and he next made his way to the Etruscan city of Clusium where Lars Porsena was King. He managed to persuade this powerful monarch to support him, and before long Rome was again under attack from an invading army. The Romans realized that this time the struggle would be long and hard. Everyone prepared for a siege as the Etruscan army made camp just a short distance from the city.

The weakest point in Rome's defences was the wooden bridge

across the Tiber which allowed soldiers and supplies to move in and out of the city. This bridge was guarded day and night by groups of hand-picked soldiers who had orders to destroy it if, by any chance, the Etruscans came too close.

Soon after the battle for Rome had begun, an alarming event took place. The two armies were fighting outside the city walls when the Etruscans suddenly broke through the Roman lines. Instead of regrouping for a counter-attack, the Romans fled and ran in panic towards the bridge, with the enemy close behind them. The man commanding the soldiers on the bridge that day was Horatius Cocles and he saw at once that Rome could only be saved by prompt action. 'Men,' he cried, 'do not desert your posts now and leave the way open to the Etruscans. You must destroy the bridge, but in the name of all the gods be quick!'

The men took up axes, saws and crowbars to begin the task of dismantling the bridge while Horatius, his shield and sword at the ready, dashed to the further end of the bridge, prepared to hold back the approaching enemy. There he stood, one man against an army of thousands. The Etruscans were so surprised by his sudden act of bravery that at first no-one moved forward to challenge him.

Then Horatius was joined by two other soldiers, Spurius Lartius and Titus Herminius, who were ashamed to leave their comrade to face such danger alone. The three men withstood the attacks of the best and bravest of the enemy, defeating everyone who came against them. When the Etruscans saw how easily their warriors were cut down by the fierce young Romans they were afraid.

Suddenly there were shouts from the men dismantling the bridge. The last few timbers were giving way and already the bridge was swaying. Horatius commanded his companions to retreat. They darted back across the bridge to safety, feeling the timbers break behind as they went. Only Horatius, blind to the danger that surrounded him, remained at his post. The Etruscans saw their chance and surged forward, hoping to cross the bridge before it was too late. Defiantly, Horatius fought them off one by one

at the narrow entrance to the bridge. The sheer weight of numbers threatened to push him back, but still he held his ground until, with a great crash, the bridge finally gave way and fell into the surging waters of the Tiber. The Romans gave a shout of triumph.

It seemed that the fate of Horatius was sealed for with the bridge in ruins, escape was impossible. He turned and looked across at the city he had risked his life to defend, then with a prayer to Father Tiber he leaped, still fully armed, into the water. The men on both sides waited to see if he would reappear. Eventually the crest of his helmet was seen above the waves, then his arms. He swam desperately against the current, the weight of his armour repeatedly pulling him under. At last, to his great relief, he felt solid earth beneath his feet and the willing hands of friends helping him up the river bank. Triumphantly they carried him into the city, accompanied by crowds of cheering people. To show their gratitude the Senate ordered a statue of Horatius to be set up and also gave him a portion of land as a reward.

In the weeks and months which followed Lars Porsena continued his siege, determined to make the Romans submit simply by starving them. The Romans suffered great hardship and the situation was desperate when a man named Gaius Mucius thought of a possible way to drive Lars Porsena and his Etruscan army away. He went to a meeting of the Senate with a simple request.
'I wish to cross the river,' he announced, 'and enter the enemy camp in disguise. I cannot tell you what I hope to do, but if my plan works the honour and glory of Rome will be increased.'

The senators agreed to the request and Mucius set off. Once in the enemy camp he mingled with the crowds and worked his way to the place where the King stood with his courtiers and army commanders. Mucius had never seen Lars Porsena at close quarters and was unable to distinguish him with certainty from those around him since they were all dressed in a similar way. He knew that he had to risk choosing the wrong man as he sprang forward, pulling out the dagger which he had hidden in his clothing. Before anyone could stop him he

had used the weapon with deadly effect and a man lay lifeless at his feet. Almost at once he realized his mistake for he was siezed and dragged before the King, who was still very much alive. Lars Porsena was furious.

'Who are you?' he shouted. 'And why have you killed my secretary, a man whom I love and trust.'

Mucius stood his ground fearlessly.

'I am a Roman,' he declared, 'and I came here to kill you, since you are Rome's enemy. Unfortunately I made a mistake, but the next Roman who comes will be more successful. You must be on your guard every hour of every day, for more will follow me. From now on this is how the war will be fought.'

The King was afraid as well as angry.

'Tell me about these others. I shall have you tortured unless you give me the information.'

'I shall tell you nothing,' replied Mucius.

'Have you no fear of torture?' asked Lars Porsena.

In reply Mucius calmly turned round and placed his right hand in a fire that was burning nearby. He held it there without showing any sign of pain until the guards pulled him away. His action greatly impressed the Etruscan King.

'You are free,' he said. 'I cannot keep such a courageous man a prisoner any longer.'

'I am grateful for my freedom,' replied Mucius, 'and I will tell you now what I should never have told under torture. I am but one of three hundred men in Rome, all sworn to try to kill you. Each will take his chance, just as I have done, until eventually we succeed.'

Lars Porsena allowed Mucius to return to Rome and soon after, envoys arrived in the city with his plans for peace. The brave scheme of Mucius had succeeded for Lars Porsena felt he could no longer continue the siege when he was personally threatened by men as desperate and brave as Mucius. Terms for peace were agreed and the Etruscans withdrew, leaving generous supplies of food for the starving Romans.

Tarquin's attempt to regain the throne by force had failed and Rome was a free Republic once more. Gaius Mucius was rewarded for his part in saving the city and because his right hand had been so badly burned that he could no longer use it, he became known affectionately as 'Mucius the left-handed'.

This was not the only occasion when Rome was saved by reason rather than by force of arms. Before many years had passed the city was again at war, this time against the Volscians. These people had been on bad terms with the Romans for a long time and their dislike was stirred up anew when the Roman Coriolanus arrived in their city. Coriolanus had been a great general and a leading member of the Senate but had become involved in a bitter quarrel over the way in which the city should be governed. His enemies arranged for him to be brought to trial and he was accused of crimes against the people and condemned to leave Rome for ever. Sadly, he found refuge with the Volscians.

More than anything else, Coriolanus longed for revenge and he persuaded the Volscians to arm and march against Rome. With Coriolanus as one of its commanders, the Volscian army successfully captured large areas of Roman territory and eventually made camp before the great city itself.

Inside Rome there was fear and confusion. No-one wanted another war and envoys were sent to ask for peace. Coriolanus refused to co-operate. He was determined to conquer Rome.

This time it was the women of Rome who thought of a way to save their city from disaster. Coriolanus had not taken his old mother or his wife and children with him when he had left Rome. They still lived there and were persuaded by the people to go to see Coriolanus as nothing else would move him.

Soon a long, silent procession of black-clad women was seen leaving the city. At its head walked the mother of Coriolanus, bent and crippled with age, while his wife and two small sons followed behind. When Coriolanus realized who they were he ran forward to greet them, but they sadly turned away as he approached, refusing to talk to him. He could see that they were suffering because of him and at last he understood how they felt. To his family he was a beloved son, husband and father who was threatening their home; to them and to the other silent women he was also a son of Rome, come to destroy the city that had formed him. 'Return to your home,' he said quietly. 'Rome is safe, for from this moment my anger is dead.'

He kissed each member of his family in turn and the procession returned silently along the road to Rome. With a sad and troubled heart Coriolanus led the Volscian army away, never to see his home or his family again.

The rise of Rome

The stories and legends which the ancient Romans told about their warrior heroes give a vivid picture of a city growing in power, testing its strength against its neighbours and gradually building the reputation for courage and honour which later Romans were to value so highly. One of the heroes of the early republic was an army commander named Camillus.

A hundred years after the final defeat of Tarquin, Rome was again at war against the Etruscans. It had been decided to attack the richest of the enemy's cities, a place called Veii. The Romans had been trying to capture it for ten years without success and Camillus was determined that it would fall while he was in command. To encourage his troops, he promised a generous share of the city's wealth to everyone who helped to win it. He also asked the gods for their help, promising them rich gifts for their temples in return for their support.

Camillus' new plan was to take the city by surprise and he ordered the digging of a tunnel to go under the walls and eventually up into the centre of the city. Work continued day and night, unseen by the enemy, until all was ready. Then soldiers moved in to attack the walls while others crept in through the tunnel to break out in the heart of the city, where the temple of Juno stood. Attacked from both the front and the rear, Veii was soon overwhelmed and the Romans rushed in, looting and destroying everything they could find. The people were sold into slavery and all their wealth was taken to Rome.

Camillus had promised his gods rich rewards for their help and he now arranged for all the precious contents of the Etruscan temples to be removed. The treasuries were carefully emptied so that their contents could be taken to Rome and the images and statues of the gods were reverently packed onto wagons for their journey. Extra care was taken with the statue of Juno, the city's special goddess. A team of young men was chosen to move it and before they entered the temple, they bathed all over and dressed in clean white gowns. As they stood looking up at the magnificent statue, deciding how best to handle it, they were suddenly afraid to touch it, it was so sacred. Then, it is said, one of the young men plucked up courage and spoke to the goddess.

'Great Queen of Heaven,' he said, 'is it your wish to go to Rome?'

Again they looked up and this time they all saw the statue nod its head very gently. Despite its great size, the statue was light to carry and the journey was made quickly and easily. Obviously, they said, the goddess was eager to see her new home.

After his success at Veii, Camillus took his army to another Etruscan stronghold, the city of Falerii. Like Veii, it showed no sign of weakening and both sides waited for the other to give way, each determined not to be the first to retreat. Then something most unexpected happened and brought an early victory to the Romans.

There was in Falerii a schoolmaster who used to take his class of boys out for walks beyond the city walls to make sure that they had plenty of exercise. The boys he taught were the sons of the city's leading statesmen but the fact that a war was in progress and that they might be in danger made no difference to the schoolmaster. One day he took them out as usual and ventured much farther than before, walking all the way to the Roman camp. He went straight to the place where Camillus had his headquarters and boldly walked into the commander's tent.
'What are you doing here?' asked Camillus when he saw the unexpected visitors. 'We are your enemies. What do you want with us?'

The schoolmaster calmly replied, 'I have brought you the sons of all the leading men of Falerii. Keep them as your hostages and you will have the city at your mercy.'
'What a low opinion you must have of me and my countrymen,' said Camillus. 'We do not stoop to such tricks, and neither should you. You are a scoundrel.'

Then he ordered the man to be stripped of his clothes and to have his hands tied behind him. Each boy was given a stick and told to beat the teacher all the way back to school. An excited crowd gathered to watch the noisy procession and soon everyone in the city knew what had happened. The Etruscans were full of admiration for Camillus for acting in such a just and honourable way and for refusing an easy victory. Realizing that if all Romans behaved in this way

they would make better friends than enemies, the people began to demand peace with Rome and an end to the war. A peace treaty was signed with no further blood lost on either side and the army returned to Rome in triumph.

For a time Camillus' reputation was high but not long afterwards, there was a serious quarrel among the leaders of the Roman people and he was forced to leave the city and make his home in the city of Ardea. At about the same time a strange voice was heard in Rome, speaking words of warning.
'Romans, prepare yourselves,' it said, 'for the Gauls are coming.'
'The Gauls,' scoffed the leaders, 'how can they threaten us? They are mere barbarians. How can they travel so far?'

The Romans were wrong, however, for already hordes of Gallic tribesmen had crossed the Alps and attacked cities in the north of Italy. Although they were less highly trained than the Italian soldiers, the tribesmen were fierce warriors who loved battle and bloodshed; many armies fled simply at the sight of them.

News soon arrived in Rome that the Gauls were marching towards the city, their straggling lines of horsemen spread wide across miles of the countryside. The Roman army marched out to meet them but their task was hopeless. In a short time they had been pushed back in disorder, leaving the way open to the city itself. Everyone in Rome panicked, for now escape seemed impossible. Those who were young and healthy took the treasures of the city and what food they could find, and took up residence on the Capitol Hill which was known as the Citadel. Many fled from their homes and took refuge in the surrounding countryside, while those who were too old or weak to move stayed at home to await the enemy with true Roman courage.

When the Gauls finally arrived, they found the gates open and the city empty and deserted. Ruthlessly they began to destroy everything they could find, smashing statues and tearing down temples and houses as they searched for gold, jewels and money. The people sheltering on the Citadel watched while their city was ransacked and then set on fire, quite unable to prevent its destruction. All they could do was to send an urgent message to Camillus in Ardea in a last desperate hope that he would be able to save what was left of the great city of Rome.

When most of Rome had been destroyed, the Gauls made their camp around the base of the Citadel, determined that none of the Romans trapped there should escape. One night, however, they discovered a way up the steep side of the hill and decided to attack this last stronghold. Silently the barbarians began to scale the steep side of the hill, gradually working their way up to the very top while the Romans slept.

Within the Citadel's walls stood a great temple dedicated to Juno and there lived a large flock of geese, birds which were sacred to the goddess. As the unsuspecting Romans slept on, the geese began to stir at the stealthy sounds of clambering footsteps on the rock. When the Gauls climbed the fortress walls the geese attacked, stretching their necks low along the ground, hissing and clacking noisily, flapping their wings to frighten the intruders. The guards woke instantly at the noise and rushed to defend the walls, catching the barbarian soldiers unawares in their turn and

hurtling them down to certain death on the rocks far below.

The geese had saved the Citadel of Rome and from that time on they were guarded even more carefully by the priests of Juno. Never again, they decreed, should a sacred bird be sacrificed, but they should all live their lives out in peace.

A few days later Camillus appeared with a strong army. The Gauls were defeated and as the people began the slow task of rebuilding their city, they honoured Camillus as another Romulus, a second founder of Rome.

Heroes and Emperors

After the destruction of the city by the Gauls, the story of Rome becomes more a matter of history and less of legend. The city and its surrounding territory recovered from the attack, leaving the Romans with all their old ambitions. They renewed their campaign of conquest and as the years passed they conquered not only the whole of Italy but also most of the lands around the Mediterranean Sea.

The age of Kings had gone for ever but the Republic, established after the reign of Tarquin the Proud had come to an end, remained for hundreds of years as the means by which Rome and her growing territories were governed. However, the Republic underwent many changes and was constantly threatened by powerful and ambitious men.

Eventually, about half way through the first century BC two great generals, Pompey and Julius Caesar, shared almost total power. In the struggle which ensued Pompey was defeated but before Julius Caesar could gain absolute power for himself he was stabbed to death by a group of his enemies on the Ides of March in 44 BC. Another deadly struggle for control followed his murder. This time the contestants were Octavian and Mark Anthony. After years of argument and intrigue Mark Anthony was defeated at the battle of Actium in 31 BC.

With the victory of Octavian the Republic came to an end, for the man who was now master of the Roman world became its first Emperor.

Octavian was given the title of Augustus, meaning 'the revered', the one who has divine approval, and from what we know of his actions, he seems to have lived up to his name. After years of bitter civil war, he brought a much-needed time of peace and order to the Empire. He had been ruthless in his rise to power but once in command he began an ambitious programme of reforms. His aim was to revive all the good things from the old Republican system so that Rome could rise to new greatness in the future.

One of Augustus' main tasks, he believed, was to restore both the old virtues of the Roman people and also their religion. Not only had temples been neglected and left to fall down, but all the traditional observances and rituals of the state cult had been allowed to lapse.

Many believed that this widespread neglect had led to the suffering and disaster which marked the end of the Republic. It was said that the fortunes of Rome would improve if the gods were properly worshipped. For his part Augustus built or rebuilt temples in many places, but mainly in Rome. He also re-established a thriving priesthood and eventually accepted for himself the post of *pontifex maximus* or chief priest.

Augustus not only revived the interest of his people in the traditional gods and in the ancient rituals, he also promoted many of the Greek deities such as Apollo and Diana, so that the religion of the new age should appeal to men of many races. The gods were not to be the gods of Rome, or of Italy alone, but of the whole Empire.

During the time of Augustus there was a widespread belief in the traditional idea that the life of the world was divided up into periods or ages. Many people believed prophecies which foretold that a new age of happiness, peace and prosperity was about to begin. Indeed, since the signs were all about them, it seemed to people that this Golden Age had in fact already dawned. To commemorate this new beginning and to express the great revival of devotion to the gods Augustus organized a very impressive celebration. It was held in Rome in 17 BC and consisted of nine days of elaborate ritual, led by the Emperor himself as chief priest. The ceremonies took place amid the newly built and decorated temples and were accompanied by processions and singing. Afterwards, in the traditional manner, there were games to entertain and amuse the people. The whole event was obviously very impressive and did much to promote the image of Augustus as the one who had restored a good relationship between men and the powers of heaven.

It was just a short step to the belief that the Emperor was a god himself. In Egypt and other parts of the ancient East there was a very long-standing tradition of kings being worshipped as gods. When these eastern lands became part of the mighty Roman Empire it was quite natural for their peoples to think of the Emperor in just the same way. In Rome, however, the idea was completely unacceptable and Augustus was always careful not to claim divinity for himself. Nevertheless, he did call himself *Divi filius*—the son of a god—because he was the adopted son of Julius Caesar.

To strengthen his own position as a chosen leader of the Roman people, Julius Caesar had in his lifetime claimed direct descent from the goddess Venus. He obviously believed that he was himself divine and therefore ideally suited for the task of controlling the destiny of Rome! After his death, the Senate officially confirmed his divinity. One story tells how Venus tried everything in her power to prevent him from being murdered, even hiding him in a cloud so that his enemies could not find him. Caesar's death, however, had already been decreed by the Fates, so Jupiter suggested she should rescue his soul as he died and change it into a star.

As Venus carried the soul upwards through the air, she felt it grow warmer and warmer until it caught fire and flew away from her. It soared upwards, changing miraculously into a comet with a long, fiery tail. From his place in the heavens the divine Caesar looked down on Rome and on the greatness and glory of his son Augustus.

People were allowed, even encouraged, to worship the genius or 'guardian spirit' of the Emperor Augustus, but not the man himself, at least not until after his death. Of the later Emperors some followed the example of Augustus, while others, unwisely, allowed their subjects to believe in their divinity. The Emperor Caligula was convinced of his own divinity and immortality and dedicated a temple to himself which contained a life-sized statue finished in pure gold. Later the Emperor Vespasian is reported to have joked about the idea of divinity, for when he knew that he was dying he said, laughing, 'I think I'm becoming a god!'

However, it seems that what began as a way of gaining the loyalty and devotion of the people gradually became just part of the mighty Roman political machine.

The age of Augustus was a time of taking stock, of looking not only to the future but also to the past. There was great interest in the beginnings of Rome. Everyone knew the story of Romulus and the she-wolf and of the events surrounding the foundation of the city of Rome, but before that the story was far from complete. There were certainly no majestic heroes in Rome's past like the ones described in Greek mythology.

It was during the time of Augustus, in the decisive years that marked the end of the Republic and the beginning of the Empire, that some of the greatest of all Roman poets lived— Ovid, Horace and Virgil—and the historian Livy. In their writings, blending history, legend, folk-tale and myth, the heroic story of Rome and its founders was gradually retold, with gods and heroes playing their parts in a history made worthy of the Emperor Augustus and his Golden Age.

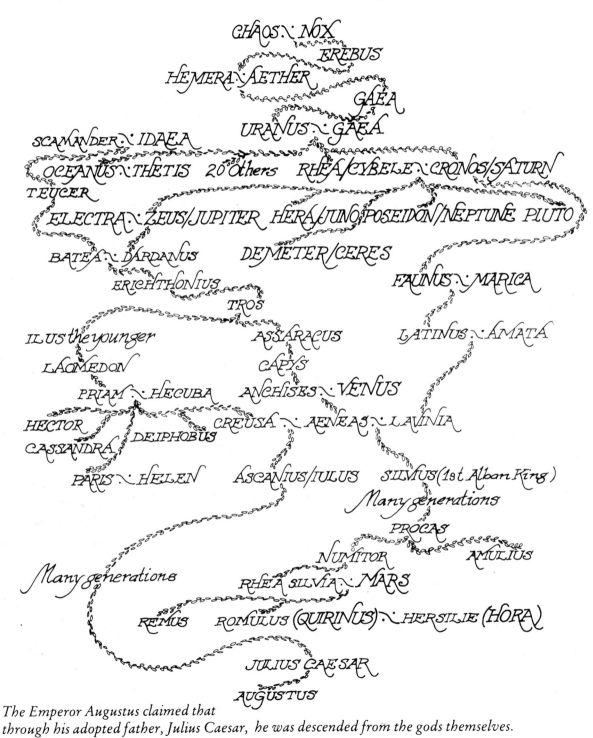

The Emperor Augustus claimed that through his adopted father, Julius Caesar, he was descended from the gods themselves.

118

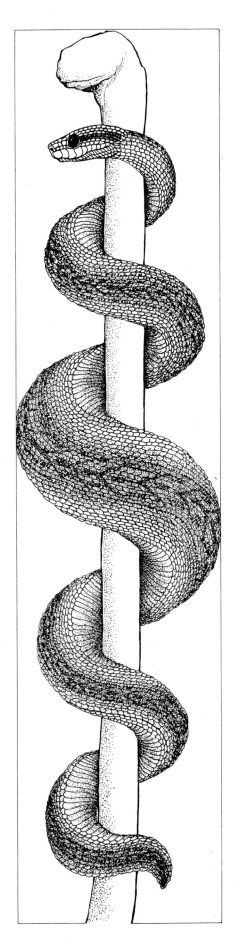

Heroes who saved Rome

The stories which follow are about characters familiar in the mythology of the Greeks but who also have a connection with the great story of Rome. All the characters were heroes: they had divine fathers and mortal mothers, but because of their outstanding deeds they eventually became gods, and all had temples built in their honour in Rome.

Hercules, probably the greatest of the ancient heroes, was known to the Greeks as Herakles. Their stories tell how he was persecuted throughout his life by the goddess Hera (Juno) simply because he was the son of her husband Zeus (Jupiter) and a mortal girl Alcmene. His first heroic deed was to strangle two snakes sent by Hera to destroy him while he was still a baby and throughout his life he continued to perform amazing feats of strength. As a young man he was placed by Hera under the command of Eurystheus and ordered to perform a series of strenuous tasks or labours. These included the slaying of a very fierce lion and of a nine-headed monster, obtaining the Amazon Queen's girdle and the golden apples of the Hesperides, and also bringing Cerberus, the three-headed dog, from the Underworld. It was while Hercules was engaged in another great task, the capturing of the oxen of a three-headed, six-armed giant named Geryon, that he came to the future site of the city of Rome. There, quite by accident, his strength and courage were again put to the test.

When Aeneas first visited King Evander he found him celebrating a festival in honour of Hercules. Evander lived with his people at the place beside the river Tiber where Rome was built in later times. Their devotion to Hercules was due to the fact that some years earlier the hero had saved them from a terrible monster.

This monster, called Cacus, lived in a nearby cave cut deep into the mountainside. He was the son of the fire-god Vulcan and for that reason was able to breathe flames and smoke from his great mouth. He was half-human, half-animal but of enormous size and with a great appetite for flesh, especially the flesh of men. The mouth of his cave was littered with the remains of his meals and soaked with the blood of his victims.

The people were becoming really desperate, for alone they could not hope to kill the creature. It was then that Hercules appeared, driving a great herd of oxen, the prize he had won for defeating Geryon. He stopped for the night below the seven hills of Rome so that the animals could drink from the river and rest there.

From his cave Cacus heard the lowing of the oxen and he longed for the hearty meal that just one of those beasts would provide. His longing soon became a mad frenzy of desire. Besides, to steal oxen from the mighty Hercules was a temptation he could not resist. While Hercules slept, Cacus stole four of his finest animals and dragged them by their tails back to his lair, cunningly covering all traces of their hoofmarks as he went. Once inside his cave the greedy monster hid the oxen then watched as Hercules awoke and prepared to leave. The hero did not bother to count his herd so had no idea that a thief had been busy.

As the cattle moved slowly forward they began to call to one another, making the countryside resound with their lowing. Faintly but clearly came the answering calls of the four animals imprisoned by Cacus. At once Hercules realized what had happened and was gripped by a terrible rage. He seized his heavy club and strode purposefully towards the entrance of the monster's cave. Cacus, who was out fetching water from a spring, saw him coming and for the first time in his life he felt terrified. Usually he moved slowly because of his great bulk, but now fear spurred him to make for his home with remarkable speed. Vulcan had hung a huge rock above the entrance of the cave, fixed by a clamp of iron, and only to be released in case of real danger. Quickly Cacus broke the clamp. The stone crashed down, blocking the doorway, but only just in time. Hercules pulled and wrenched at it, trying to get in, but even he was unable to shift it. Then, angrier than ever, he stormed three times round the mountain, seeking a place to break in. Three times he had to give up, exhausted.

Then Hercules looked up and saw, at the very top of the mountain, a sharp pinnacle of rock which was used as a nesting place by birds of prey. With renewed strength he climbed the steep side of the mountain and, grasping the pinnacle, began to work it backwards and forwards until gradually he managed to loosen

it. At last he tore it away and in triumph threw it crashing down, making the earth tremble and the river stop in its course. A huge opening appeared where the pinnacle had been and looking through it Hercules could see Cacus cowering in a corner of his den. The monster looked up into the glare of daylight to see the face of his angry enemy who was already throwing rocks and uprooted trees down into the cavern.

Cacus cried out in fear and pain. He was too far below to fight back so instead he belched from his mouth first sheets of flame, then clouds of thick black smoke which soon filled the inside of the cave. Hercules acted swiftly. He clambered down through the smoke, making for the heart of the fire, where he knew Cacus would be. Grabbing the monster firmly, he tied his arms and legs into a knot, then seized his throat and held it until no life remained. When Cacus lay quite still, Hercules broke open the doorway of the cave and dragged out the corpse. The people gathered round it to look at the horrible sight. They saw the staring eyes, the twisted limbs and throat, the gruesome mouth blackened with smoke and ash, and they shuddered to think what danger they had escaped. Slowly they realized that they were free at last and turned gratefully to thank Hercules for his assistance.

As for Hercules, when he had rescued his four stolen oxen from the shattered remains of the cave, he set out once more to drive the herd home to the palace of Eurystheus in Greece. He never returned to the site of Rome but he was not forgotten there. On the very day that he killed the monster, the people built an altar in his honour and each year a celebration was held there to commemorate his mighty deed.

In the old days, people knew very little about the causes of disease although they understood and used a variety of herbal medicines and were able to treat many everyday illnesses. As with other events that they could not explain, they linked disease and recovery with supernatural powers and often relied on the gods miraculously to heal the sick.

During the earliest days of Rome, the city was once overwhelmed by a terrible plague. The sickness spread so quickly that the doctors could do nothing and as the situation became worse it was decided that the help of the gods must be sought. Several of those who had escaped the disease and who were fit enough to travel were sent to the shrine of Phoebus Apollo at Delphi in Greece to consult the famous oracle and to appeal to the god to save Rome from the plague. Apollo heard the prayers and caused the ground to tremble as he spoke through his prophetess. 'Romans,' said her voice from the depths of the shrine, 'it is my son Aesculapius whom you need to help you. Go from here and seek him.'

Aesculapius was the son of the god Apollo and a king's daughter named Coronis. Coronis died before giving birth to her child, but Apollo managed to snatch his baby son from the funeral pyre and, miraculously still alive, he was taken to be brought up by a wise centaur, Chiron. There he learned the arts of surgery and medicine and he was worshipped in both Greece and Rome as the god of healing.

In the ancient world anyone who wanted to appeal to him went to Epidaurus, in Greece, where he had his principal shrine. The Romans therefore sailed on to Epidaurus and, once there, met the elders of the temple to ask if the god could use his influence to bring relief to the Italians. Many of the Greeks were reluctant to allow the power of Aesculapius to be used in a foreign country and they made various excuses, hoping to deter the visitors from consulting the god. That night, however, while the Romans slept, Aesculapius appeared to them in their dreams as he often did to those who came to his shrine seeking help. It was as if he stood by their beds, stroking his long grey beard with one hand and clutching his rough wooden staff in the other. Around the staff was wound a snake, the sign of prophecy and of recovery of health and strength.

Aesculapius spoke gently to them: 'Do not be afraid. I have heard your desperate request and I shall come to Rome. I shall come disguised as my snake; look at it closely so that you may recognize it later. It will be like this but much larger.'

The god disappeared and they awoke to find the light of day streaming in through the window. Already the Epidaureans had assembled in the temple and were at prayer, beseeching the god to give them a sign to show them what he intended to do. By the time the Romans arrived at the temple the ground had begun to shake and the air was filled with a loud hissing sound. This was the prayed-for sign; their god appeared in the guise of a giant snake, its eyes burning like fire, its huge body erect. The worshippers were terrified and were on the point of running away in panic when the priest called out, 'This is the god! We must be silent in his presence and worship him so that he may bless us.'

Everyone obeyed at once. The snake swayed and bowed, then hissed before sliding out of the temple, down the steps and across the courtyard, which had been strewn with flowers in its honour. Making its way through the town the snake eventually arrived at the harbour and there slithered on board the Italian ship. The vessel sank low in the water under the weight of the great creature and seemed almost too small to contain it.

The Romans were so happy at this good fortune that they sacrificed a bull on the beach before untying the ship and sailing away on the long journey back to Rome. The cargo was an awkward one, for the serpent had to lie in vast coils within the ship, its neck resting on the stern and its head over the edge so that it looked down into the watery depths as they sailed along.

At last the ship reached the mouth of the Tiber and made its way up the river towards the city. Those who were not lying ill at home flocked to the banks of the river to greet the god. Incense burned and crackled on a thousand altars along the ship's route and the pungent smell of smoke filled the air.

As soon as the ship had been moored the giant creature reared up its head to look about and choose a suitable place to land. Then it slithered into the water, coil upon coil unwinding as it went. The people watched in silent amazement as it re-emerged on an island in mid-stream. Once there, the snake took on for an instant the shape of the god Aesculapius, then promptly disappeared from human sight. From that day the plague left Rome and its citizens enjoyed perfect health.

121

A shrine was established on the island in honour of the god, and like many of the places where Aesculapius was worshipped it became a sort of hospital where sick people gathered in the hope of being healed. The island itself was carved into the shape of a ship as a reminder of the way in which the god had been brought to Rome.

With Aesculapius were worshipped his wife Epione (the Soother) and his daughter Hygieia (the goddess of Health). When people visited the shrine they prayed and sacrificed before going to sleep in a place nearby. In their dreams the god visited them and explained how they could find a cure for their illnesses. Snakes were always regarded as the sacred servants of Aesculapius because their habit of sloughing their skins each year came to symbolize the renewal of youth. They were also apparently used in some way in the cures, probably being used to lick the wounds and ulcers of patients.

This hospital of the sacred snake was the first to be established in Rome and, under another name, a hospital still stands on the same site today.

Two other hero gods who were worshipped in ancient Greece and Rome were Castor and Pollux, the twin sons of Leda, Queen of Sparta and the great god Jupiter. Castor became famous as a horse-tamer while his brother Pollux gained a reputation as a fine boxer. After many adventures on earth they died and, as a reward for their faithful brotherly love, were set in the sky as the constellation of Gemini—the Twins.

Castor and Pollux were known in many parts of the Mediterranean: the Spartans believed that they fought with them in their battles, while seamen always prayed for their help during storms at sea. Their worship seems to have reached Italy, too, for they were favourite gods among many of the tribes there from earliest times. Like the Spartans and the Greeks, the Romans worshipped them as protectors of seamen.

There is one famous story about how the divine twins fought with the Romans at the Battle of Regillus. At the time the Romans were struggling to defeat a strong enemy army. Just when the fighting was at its fiercest and when the

Roman troops were in desperate need of encouragement Castor and Pollux appeared in the thick of the battle, their white horses and white armour gleaming in the sunlight. With these two hero-gods to help them the Romans quickly defeated their enemy.

At home in the city, the people were waiting anxiously for news of the battle when the same two shining horsemen appeared, riding side by side through the city and into the Forum. They stopped before the temple of Vesta, the hearth-goddess, dismounted and washed their horses in the sacred spring that flowed nearby. When they had finished they remounted, rode to the door of the temple and then disappeared as suddenly as they had come.

The people of Rome recognized that this strange appearance was a sign not only that the battle was won, but that the twin gods had come to give their continuing support to the city and would always be ready to help the Romans in their hour of need. A temple to Castor and Pollux was built in the Forum, next to the temple of Vesta, and from that time they were given all the honours due to the gods of Rome.

Tales of transformation

The theme of the stories in this chapter is 'change', for in each one a transformation takes place. In the first tale, Vertumnus, god of the changing seasons, is able to change his appearance at will. In the second, the Sibyl's changing form is not entirely of her own choosing and shows how cautiously even prophets must interpret the promises of the gods. The third story concerns the way in which sadness, disappointment, anger—and magic—all have the power to bring changes into peoples' lives and, lastly, there is an account of the changes that are expected when a new Golden Age begins.

The wood nymph Pomona lived long ago in the countryside outside the shining city of Alba Longa. Unlike most other nymphs, she had no love for the wild woodland. Her greatest delight was in the cultivation of apple trees, and to that she gave her wholehearted devotion. She was never happier than when she was pruning or grafting or watering her trees. She even fenced her orchard so that no man should come near to woo her and disturb her peace.

However, it was not just mortal men that she feared. She was even more afraid of the attacks of the satyrs and fauns, the spirits of the hills and woods, who were all eager for her attention. She was young and beautiful so, not surprisingly, she was much loved and admired. Among those who gazed at her with affection was the young god Vertumnus, the ruler of the year's changing seasons. It was not just the seasons that changed at his bidding for he could also change himself into a variety of forms and disguises. This he frequently did in order to approach his beloved Pomona. He found any excuse to be near her for he liked nothing better than looking at her and talking to her and longed above all to make her his wife.

Little did Pomona realize that it was the same admirer who called on her, disguised on different occasions as a ploughman, a harvester, a vine-dresser and a fruit-picker. Vertumnus even appeared one day as a soldier and on another as a fisherman. His disguises were endless, but he never appeared in his own shape.

One autumn day when the fruit hung heavily on the apple boughs Vertumnus had a new idea. He took on the shape of an old woman and hobbled into the orchard. After admiring the fruits she turned her attention, of course, to the nymph herself.

'You are far more beautiful than these apples you love so much,' she remarked, as she sat on the grass close to Pomona, holding her hand in a very affectionate manner. Then she began to talk about marriage, telling her that of all the spirits who desired to be her husband, Vertumnus was the most suitable, for he was more virtuous and more steadfast in his love than any of the others could ever be. Besides, he had more to offer as the changer of the seasons.

'Just imagine,' said the old woman persuasively, 'he can easily take on any shape you choose: you can order him to change into anything you need and he will do whatever you command. Not that he needs to change his appearance, for he is a fine young man, as handsome as any girl could wish. Besides, you both love the same things for he is the first to admire your garden, the first to praise its fruits.'

When Pomona was still unmoved, the old woman told her the story of a hard-hearted princess who rejected her lover so harshly that he hanged himself in despair. 'Remember that Venus hates hard-hearted people above everything else,' she cautioned. 'She punishes them without mercy. The girl I'm telling you about was turned into a statue as hard as her heart. You can still see it in the temple at Salamis if you don't believe me.'

Despite Vertumnus' pleading, Pomona remained unconvinced. At last, in desperation, Vertumnus shook off his disguise to stand before her in his own form for the first time, a shining god with eyes radiant with love. He was full of such passionate feelings that he was almost ready to carry her off without her consent but, to his surprise and delight she was quite overwhelmed by his beauty and by his obvious love for her. In an instant they had fallen into each other's arms and from that time on, they lived happily together as husband and wife.

The strange figure of the Sibyl Deiphobe, the priestess of Apollo and Diana, appears in many of the stories of Roman mythology. She is Aeneas' guide in his journey to the Underworld and she appears again in the story of Tarquin the Proud, offering to sell her nine books of prophecy to the King. Her prophecies, thought to be the words of the god Apollo himself, were taken very seriously in the ancient world and her advice was sought on matters of both personal and national importance. Her own story is a sad one.

When she was a young girl, the god Apollo fell in love with her and begged her to be his mistress. She was not willing to grant such a favour to anyone, not even to a god, but he persisted and promised to give her anything she wished for, in the hope of persuading her to change her mind. Looking around, she happened to see a mound of sand and suddenly she knew what she wanted.

'My wish is to live as many years as there are grains of sand in that heap,' she said.

Apollo granted her wish but still she refused him. Angrily he turned to her. 'I have granted your wish,' he told her, 'but there is one thing you have not asked for: you have forgotten to ask for eternal youth to go with all those years. Yet if you will come with me and be my love, I will make you young forever.'

'Never,' replied the Sibyl proudly. 'Let me grow old alone, if that is your condition.'

So the girl who could have been a goddess was destined to live out her long life as an ageing mortal. Already when she met Aeneas she was seven hundred years old and as time went on, she was to grow smaller and more withered until nothing was left but her tiny voice, speaking the words of prophecy. Then even Apollo would glance towards her without seeing her and would deny that he had ever loved or cherished her.

But still her voice remained to eternity, passing the words of the gods to the human world.

Witchcraft, sorcery and shape-changing were familiar themes in the country tales of old Italy. This story is set in the countryside where Aeneas first landed, before the foundation of Rome.

The old god Saturn had a son who lived long ago in ancient Latium. His name was Picus and he was so handsome that every mortal girl and every nymph fell in love with him at first sight. The dryads from the hills and woods, the nymphs from the fountains, streams and rivers, all found young Picus so attractive that he could have taken any one of them as a wife. Instead he chose to fall in love with the daughter of the

double-headed god Janus, who was a close neighbour at the time.

The girl's name was Canens and, though she was certainly beautiful to look at, her real charm lay in her singing voice. When she sang all nature listened; rocks wept, trees swayed, wild beasts grew gentle, rivers stopped flowing and birds nearly fell from the air at the sound. Janus thought Picus a most suitable match for his daughter and soon they were married.

One day while Canens was singing happily at home, Picus decided to go hunting for wild boar in the nearby forest. He was a fine horseman and looked splendid sitting on his charger holding two spears in his hand. He wore a red cloak round his shoulders, fastened with a gold brooch and rode eagerly across the fields then through the trees, his companions following behind.

At the time the goddess Circe was wandering in the depths of the forest in search of rare herbs and flowers. Circe was the daughter of Helios, the old sun-god, and was skilled in all the magic arts. She was even said to have the power to change people into animals. When she heard horses galloping towards her she looked up and saw Picus at the head of the chase. One glimpse was enough: immediately she felt a strange faintness overcoming her and she dropped her collection of precious herbs and flowers, her face burning hot but her limbs as cold as ice. Her one desire was to tell Picus at once how much she loved him, but when she called out to him her voice was lost among the trees. In desperation she decided to use her magic powers to trap the young man, so she quickly moulded a boar from the shadows and sent it running in front of the horsemen, where Picus was sure to see it.

Everything happened as Circe had planned. Picus saw the boar and followed it with a shout, believing it to be a real beast. He plunged into the thickest part of the forest, seeing his prey always just a little way ahead. Eventually the undergrowth became so thick that the horse could go no further. Picus leaped to the ground and followed on foot, blind to the dangers all about him.

Circe then used her spells to make a thick fog which covered the whole forest in a white shroud. As she chanted her magic words the sky darkened and a swirling mist rose thickly from the ground. The sorceress knew the place where the young man was and she suddenly appeared before him and spoke gently:

'Will you favour a goddess with your love?' she asked. 'Your beauty has overwhelmed me. You are so young and so desirable. Do not be shy; take me, Circe, as your bride.'

Picus turned wildly on her. 'Whether you are goddess or mortal that cannot be, for someone else already has all my love and she will keep it, always. Leave me in peace.'

Circe was not to be rejected so easily. She spoke again, trying to persuade him, repeating her offer, but Picus would not weaken, so strong was his love for Canens. Then Circe lost her temper.

'You will regret your stupid stubbornness,' she snarled. 'I will not be rejected and scorned. You will see what I can do when I am really angry.'

Determined that Picus should never return to his beloved wife, Circe worked her magic once again. Twice she leaned her body to the east, then twice to the west. Three times she touched him with her wand, then three times she chanted her evil spell. Picus paused for a moment in horror, then turned to run from her into the bushes. As the mist swirled around him he felt himself rising from the ground and soon he was flying. His arms were beating against his sides like wings and his body was becoming covered in a thick layer of feathers. The cloak that he wore had turned into red plumage while his golden brooch made a ring of brightness around his neck. Picus had turned into a bird and was so completely transformed that nothing remained of him except his name. He had become a woodpecker, known ever afterwards by the name *Picidae* in memory of the young man he had once been. Furious at its fate, the bird flew wildly among the trees, clawing and pecking at the bark as woodpeckers have continued to do ever since that day.

Meanwhile, the other huntsmen were looking for their leader, searching the forest and calling his name repeatedly. Picus heard them but was unable to answer in a language that they could understand. When he tried to call, only a harsh, woodland cry came from his feathered throat.

Sunshine and a gentle breeze had cleared the mist, making the search easier, but still they could not find him. Instead they discovered Circe hiding among the trees and recognized her as a sorceress. The men surrounded her with spears raised, suspecting her at once of spiriting Picus away.

'Bring back our lord or we'll kill you,' they shouted.

Circe crouched before them and, before they realized what was happening, she had spun round and sprinkled each with a deadly potion. Then she called loudly on the gods of Night and on Hecate, goddess of witches, howling at the top of her voice for their assistance. The earth groaned. Trees turned white, as if touched by frost. Blood ran on the grass, the stones rumbled, dogs barked, black snakes slithered across the earth and ghosts flew silently in the quivering air. The huntsmen were shivering with fear, unable to move, and when Circe touched each with her wand they were instantly transformed into wild animals of the woods, destined to wander for ever among the forest trees.

When evening came and Picus had still not returned home Canens began to worry. She sent servants out with torches to look for her husband, but they returned without finding him. When midnight had passed the girl could stay at home no longer. She ran through the fields and woods searching everywhere for Picus. For six days and nights she wandered without food or sleep, until at last she sank exhausted beside the river Tiber. She lay there weeping, softly singing her last words of mourning until she dissolved in her own tears and simply disappeared.

Later, the gods took pity on the girl with the beautiful voice who had died for love. They changed her name from Canens to Camena and to her voice they gave immortality, for it can still be heard in the faint splashing of water in fountains everywhere.

The Golden Age was a marvellous time which, so they say, existed near the beginning of the world and which some believed would return in the future. The idea of a Golden Age appears in many mythologies. According to the Greek account man originally lived a perfect sort of life under the influence of Cronos (Saturn). That came to an end when Cronos was overthrown by his son Zeus (Jupiter) and other less perfect ages followed. The poet Ovid describes it.

He says that it was a time when there was trust between living creatures and when fear and evil were absent from the lives of men. Everyone was content with the place where they lived and no city needed a wall to defend it, for there were no enemies. War trumpets were never heard, nor the clanging of swords, nor the tramp of marching feet. Work was quite unnecessary. The land was neither ploughed nor dug, for the earth gave freely of its riches. Fruit and nuts in plenty could be gathered from the trees while milk, wine and honey were there for all. Each year had only one season and that was a gentle springtime when the south wind blew softly through the leaves and across the meadows.

Inevitably this time of peace and plenty came to an end, for the death of the old god Saturn was followed by the Age of Silver, when Jupiter reigned supreme. It was then that the year was first divided into separate seasons, forcing men to build proper houses as protection against the elements. Farming also began at the same time. It was not until the Age of Bronze that the first wars began and evil came to the affairs of men. The final Age was that of Iron, a time when good was replaced by evil and when fear, greed and hate ruled in men's hearts.

Some ancient philosophers believed that the Ages were repeated over and over again through eternity and they looked forward to the time when the Age of Iron would end and the Age of Gold return. In one of his poems, the fourth *Eclogue*, Virgil takes up this idea and writes of a Wonder-child who would be the first-born of a new Age of Gold. He foresaw that great events were about to take place. The whole world was about to change, and change for the better:
'We have reached the end of an era, for Time has come full circle and a great new age is about to begin. Justice will return to our earth as the Golden Age, the rule of Saturn, is renewed. Mankind will be freed at last from fear and from the weight of evil. Darkness will disappear as light returns to the world. The first-born of this age will be sent to us from heaven and Lucina will give her blessing with a smile.

'This child already lives in the company of the gods, so he understands all the past history of the world. He will know how to rule it in peace.
'To honour the Child's birth, nature shall produce her gifts—trailing ivy, foxgloves, Egyptian lilies and smiling acanthus. His very cradle will be entwined with soft and fragrant blossoms. Goats, their udders full of milk, will go safely home without a shepherd to drive them, while the ox will have no fear of the lion. Poison shall disappear from snake and weed alike, while plants everywhere will give out rich perfumes.

'By the time the Child reaches boyhood, the earth's great plains will be gold with ripening corn. Then wild thorn bushes will produce thick clusters of grapes and honey will run from the bark of oaks.

'However, the past and its mistakes will not be wiped out completely. Men will still sail the seas, still build walls of defence around their cities, still cultivate the land. Heroes will once again set out in quest of the Golden Fleece and the Trojan War will be fought a second time.

'When the holy Child reaches full manhood, even trading will cease. The traders' ships will be drawn up out of the sea and each land will produce everything it needs. There will be no need to plough or hoe the soil, pruning will be a forgotten craft and even the oxen can be freed from their yokes. Wool will no longer be dyed, for sheep in their pastures will grow their fleeces in a range of attractive colours: purple, yellow and red.

'The Fates have spoken already: "Run, you looms. Weave the pattern of an age to come."
'They have spoken together, announcing a destiny which cannot be changed.
'It is time for the ruler sent by Jupiter to appear, that Child so dear to all the gods. His marvellous career is about to begin. Already the whole round earth waits to greet him. See the vast lands, the deep oceans, the endless sky. They and all creation rejoice in the Golden Age that is dawning.'

Symbols in the Roman myths

p. 11 THE CITY THAT CONQUERED THE WORLD The *fasces* (bundles) were made of wooden rods enclosing an axe and were carried by an officer attending the early kings of Rome as a symbol of authority. Later, in Republican times, they were carried before senior magistrates as a symbol of the legal and administrative powers of Rome. Other elements symbolize Rome's military and engineering achievements.

p. 17 GODS OF THE FAMILY The Lares and Penates, spirits of the house and store cupboard, with snake representing the genius of the house, fire (for Vesta the hearth goddess) and symbols for the great events of family life: birth, puberty, marriage and death.

p. 19 GODS OF CITY AND STATE Top: The eagle and laurel wreath are symbols of Rome and are set in a building which represents the temples and monumental buildings which were important in Roman life and religion. In the centre is Jupiter, ruler of the Roman gods. He holds a staff of authority and a stylized thunderbolt, his personal symbol and a symbol of Rome's power. The eagle was also associated with Jupiter and Rome. The sword symbolizes Rome's military might.

p. 25 SPIRITS OF THE UNDERWORLD The butterfly represents the spirit returning to its earthly home. Flowers were placed on graves at the festival of Parentalia, on the bodies of the dead and on funeral pyres. Below is Pluto, Lord of the Underworld, in his wolf mask, symbolizing his omnivorous nature.

p. 32 THE STORY OF AENEAS The wooden horse of Troy, above Calaeno, the chief harpy and Aeneas's helmet. In the background, lightning symbolizes both the storms that hindered Aeneas's voyage and the presence of the gods. Below, the whirlpool Charybdis and the monster Scylla represent the dangers of the journey to Italy.

p. 40 DIDO AND AENEAS A Trojan storm-wrecked ship above the sheltered cove where the fleet took refuge. Below, Queen Dido of Carthage.

p. 51 THE GOLDEN BOUGH The golden bough itself is traditionally held to have been mistletoe found growing on oak—the sacred tree of Jupiter. Mistletoe rarely grows with oak and is considered sacred when it does so. Below is Charon the boatman with Cerberus, the three-headed guardian of the Underworld. Next are the shadowy spirits of the dead with, bottom, the flowers of the Elysian fields.

p. 58 WAR IN ITALY Top, the gates stand open to proclaim that war has been declared. The figure is Alecto, the Fury directly responsible for the conflict. Around her head are the bees which settled on the sacred laurel tree in Latinus's palace courtyard. Alecto holds a branch of laurel.

p. 61 THE SITE OF ROME Aeneas's armour, forged by Vulcan and the Cyclopes at Venus's request. The shield shows scenes from Rome's future.

p. 64 THE SIEGE Aeneas's soldiers guard their camp. Below, the sea goddesses, once the Trojan fleet.

p. 69 THE GREAT BATTLE The gods (Jupiter, Mars, Venus, Diana and Juno) discuss the battle. Below, Aeneas's fleet returns, with fighting figures, including the warrior-maiden Camilla.

p. 77 THE END OF THE WAR Turnus and Aeneas in single combat.

p. 80 ROMULUS AND REMUS Top, the new city of Rome on the Palatine Hill, with the twin brothers Romulus and Remus. Below is the wolf (sacred to Mars) who suckled them. Bottom, Rhea Silvia's dream of twin trees growing from her head—the twin sons she was to bear.

p. 87 THE SABINE WOMEN Mars descends to take Romulus to the home of the gods. Below, the Romans carry off the Sabine women.

p. 93 NUMA, THE WISE KING The sacred grove of Egeria. Two priests burn incense and offer libations to the gods, symbolizing the peoples' return to religion under Numa.

p. 96 THE HOUSE OF TARQUIN An eagle, symbol of the gods and the omen which told Tarquin he would be king. Behind is the Senate building and the stones which rained from the sky to call the people back to the worship of the gods.

p. 101 TARQUIN THE PROUD The Sybil with the 3 sybilline books. At her feet are the flower heads which Tarquin struck off as a signal that he wished the influential citizens of Gabii to be cut down.

p. 105 THE EARLY REPUBLIC The decorative trees and leaves stand for Sylvanus, speaking from the forests. Below is the bridge Horatius defended and Gaius Mucius holding his hand in the flames to prove his disregard of physical pain.

p. 111 THE RISE OF ROME The Citadel on Capitol Hill, with Juno's sacred geese forming a barrier between the Romans and the Gauls. The Gauls are pulling down the sacred images, symbolizing their disregard for Roman religion and the Roman state. The disordered pattern of men and horses indicates the wild nature of the barbarians, in contrast to Roman organization.

p. 116 HEROES AND EMPERORS Julius Caesar, Augustus (the first Emperor) and Caligula.

p. 119 HEROES WHO SAVED ROME The staff of Aesculapius, now the international symbol for medicine and doctors.

p. 124 TALES OF TRANSFORMATION Apples symbolize the wood nymph Pomona (her name comes from the Latin word *Pomus*, apple or fruit tree), and her love of orchards. The woodpecker is Picus, transformed by Circe. Below are flowers and animals, symbolizing the perpetual summer of the Golden Age, when all creation lived in harmony; but the small animals are also the huntsmen who accompanied Picus and who were transformed by Circe.

Index